EDITED BY C
SERIES EDITOR **TOM BENNETT**

THE research **ED** GUIDE TO

THE
CURRICULUM

....

AN EVIDENCE-INFORMED
GUIDE FOR TEACHERS

JOHN CATT

First Published 2020

by John Catt Educational Ltd,
15 Riduna Park, Station Road,
Melton, Woodbridge IP12 1QT

Tel: +44 (0) 1394 389850
Email: enquiries@johncatt.com
Website: www.johncatt.com

© **2020 John Catt Educational**

ISBN: 978 1 912906 38 3

Set and designed by John Catt Educational Limited

WHAT IS researchED?

researchED is an international, grassroots education-improvement movement that was founded in 2013 by Tom Bennett, a London-based high school teacher and author. researchED is a truly unique, teacher-led phenomenon, bringing people from all areas of education together onto a level playing field. Speakers include teachers, principals, professor, researchers and policy makers.

Since our first sell-out event, researchED has spread all across the UK, into the Netherlands, Norway, Sweden, Australia, the USA, with events planned in Spain, Japan, South Africa and more. We hold general days as well as themed events, such as researchED Maths & Science, or researchED Tech.

WHO ARE WE?

Since 2013, researchED has grown from a tweet to an international conference movement that so far has spanned six continents and thirteen countries. We have simple aims: to help teaching become more evidence-facing; to raise the research literacy in teaching; to improve education research standards; and to bring research users and research creators closer together. To do this, we hold unique one-day conferences that bring together teachers, researchers, academics and anyone touched by research. We believe in teacher voice, and short-circuiting the top-down approach to education that benefits no one.

HOW DOES IT WORK?

The gathering of mainly teachers, researchers, school leaders, policymakers and edu-bloggers creates a unique dynamic. Teachers and researchers can attend the sessions all day and engage with each other to exchange ideas. The vast majority of speakers stay for the duration of the conference, visit each other's sessions, work on the expansion of their knowledge and gain a deeper understanding of the work of their peers. Teachers can take note of recent developments in educational research, but are also given the opportunity to provide feedback on the applicability of research or practical obstacles.

PRAISE FOR THE researchED GUIDE TO THE CURRICULUM

Tim Oates

'If you listen carefully, you can hear the rumble of a long-overdue paradigm shift. A balanced, evidence-based position is emerging in curriculum theory. This book helps ensure that the shift in theory can have a supportive and helpful impact on day-to-day practice.'

Mary Myatt

'Gripping insights and terrific ideas on curricular thinking and planning. This book needs to be read by every teacher and leader, in every school, period. Also, very funny.'

CONTENTS

FOREWORD
BY TOM BENNETT

Before I trained to be a teacher, I had no idea what I was supposed to teach children. When I actually started to teach, I had *next to* no idea, which is surely an improvement but not what you might call an impressive one. I clearly remember that it was assumed we already had a robust 'bank' of knowledge to teach because we had been accepted on to the teacher training course. And that may have been the case if I had been accepted to teach mathematics on the basis of possessing a maths degree. But like so many in my position, my qualifications (a degree in philosophy, rusty from misuse) mapped awkwardly on to the subject I was training to teach – religious studies, humanities. I rapidly discovered that the ability to parse David Hume's empiricism was of fractional use to someone required to teach kosher food laws, the growth of the Church, and the five pillars of Islam. I frequently found myself a page ahead of the students, and it took me years to acquire anything approaching content competence. And here's the odd thing: no one noticed.

So what? Anecdote isn't data, or significant data by itself. But looking back, I realised that the environment I found myself in was frighteningly indifferent to content, or how it was sequenced, or curriculum, as I later learned to describe it. At school, I discovered that the sequence of lessons we taught was a patchwork quilt of topics and themes: rites of passage, the life of Jesus, moral issues, etc. Enjoyable enough, with plenty to find interesting, or make interesting, but it was a collage achieved, apparently, by opening a child's encyclopaedia and throwing darts at it. Crucially, we found ourselves reteaching things a good deal, as they had been entirely forgotten after a few months or years. Nothing fitted together. Part of the reason was the peculiar position RE occupied in the UK curriculum, which currently enjoys a skeleton framework sequence of topics across a core range of subjects (the national curriculum), but not in RE. In that subject, when I taught, the requirement was that it had to be 50% devoted to Christianity (to reflect the broadly Christian character of the UK) and the recommendation was that it be in accordance with the SACRE (a locally formed panel that designed notional curriculums for religious education). RE was compulsory, but not mandated in design. You just had to teach it. But what was 'it'? And in what order?

Years later, I can see what a profound mistake this was and how lost we were in a system where curriculum was almost seen as an afterthought: a mere description of what had been taught rather than the blueprint for how we assemble learning. Because, as this book explores, what we teach, and in what order, is enormously important. A somewhat bland point to make, one might think, but parents would probably be fascinated or shocked to learn how controversial this point is to make in education. The recent, decades-long love affair education has had with skills-based curriculums has resulted in systems that have focused on what students are expected to be able to do rather than what they are expected to know. And of course, these two aspects are inextricably linked. But getting the balance wrong leads us into some dark places.

For example, everyone wants their children to be critical thinkers, independently minded, creative and capable of wonderful collaborative acts. The problem occurs when we untether these ambitions from the content that creates the very aptitudes, skills, abilities, we aspire to inculcate. It is as if, mesmerised by castles and palaces, we neglected to bring the bricks that built them.

It is common to deride this perspective by responding that no school teaches *no* content, that no one eschews facts themselves. And that is true. But it has been, for too long, over emphasised that facts are mundane compared to the beautiful, glittering goals of transferable skills we seek.

But no longer. Happily, recent trends in education have started to push back against this paradigm. What is taught, and in what order, and to what ends, have re-emerged as topics of primary importance. The tail is no longer wagging the dog quite so easily. Great minds – some of whom write in this book – have re-ignited the conversation about the centrality of the curriculum. Better yet, they are prepared for the criticisms that this approach can entail, and have thought deeply about their responses. Academics and practitioners alike have appeared to discuss issues of disciplinary sequencing in a public way that was barely discernible to previous generations of teachers. Because this is a conversation that needs to occur between teacher-practitioners, academics, researchers, policy makers and communities. The *what* drives the *how*, which drives *how we assess*, and so on.

As with so many other areas currently being driven out of the shadows and into the spring sunshine of evidence-informed enquiry, this is an extraordinary period to watch in education. We are present at the birth of a new era in education design. And Clare Sealy has edited a fascinating guide to it, and assembled some of the midwives of this very process. If you are involved in any aspect of curriculum, I think you'll find this book tremendously useful.

INTRODUCTION

CLARE SEALY

This book is about the curriculum. That is to say it is about how we choose what it is we will teach the students in our schools and why those choices are important. Every time we choose to include something, we are also choosing *not* to include many other possibilities. The responsibility inherent in choosing some material rather than others can be intimidating. Our choices are always contestable. But choose we must. In this book, I have chosen nine authors – who have in their professional lives wrestled with the responsibility of choosing – to share with us some of their thoughts about that process. In the following chapters, some of them write about the criteria they have used in order to make choices. Others focus on how to sequence chosen material in ways more likely to be effective. All of them will, I believe, help you make more informed choices about what you will – and won't – include in your curriculum.

A few years ago, the idea of the curriculum as the prime engine of school improvement would have seemed very strange. The discourse was much more concentrated on *how* to teach, rather than on *what* to teach. The *what* was perceived as almost irrelevant.

A few years ago, I would have considered it very strange to think about the curriculum in any detail. I was much more interested in thinking about *how* to teach, rather than on *what* to teach. The *what* for some subjects was dictated from on high, via the national curriculum, or, more importantly, the statutory tests that held us to account. The tests formed the curriculum and therefore shaped what was taught. But most subjects weren't tested. So the *what* in these subjects didn't really concern me, beyond finding something that seemed interesting and, more importantly, was easy to find activities and resources for. These were the days of the activity-rich curriculum.

Yet this wasn't very satisfying. The disparity between the rigour with which we taught English and maths in the mornings and the rigour with which we taught everything else in the afternoons bothered me. I remember doing some lesson observations one afternoon – which in itself was unusual – and thinking, 'If the inspectors came today, they'd grade us as "great" in the morning and "special measures" in the afternoon.' The teaching of generic skills seemed like a promising alternative and so I signed the school up to a programme that promised to help us do just that. The idea was that children would research an area, following up their own interests, and then report what they had found in some way. We'd start the topic with some exciting event to hook the children in and draw it all together at the end with an event to showcase what they had learnt.

The problem was that both children and staff found the research aspect not only difficult, but profoundly unsatisfying. One class were tasked with finding out all about hydroelectric power. This seemed to us adults like a really interesting and important topic with its links to sustainable power generation and reducing carbon emissions. The problem was that if you don't know anything about sustainability – or different ways of generating power, or different forms of energy, or even why we need energy to do various things, or about carbon emissions, or climate change, or indeed the atmosphere, or rivers – then it very quickly ceases to be an interesting topic and becomes a very boring activity, googling facts about the Aswan Dam and writing them on a poster. Frankly, it was better when we spent the afternoons making things out of cardboard. At least that was fun. Leaving children to research their way into the subject without appreciating the need to know about all these other things first meant we were on a hiding to nothing. And we could hardly expect the children to know that they needed to teach themselves about all these other areas first, and in the right order, with some things needing to be learnt before others. What we needed to do was to teach them, bit by bit, all the different elements that went into understanding why hydroelectric power generation might be better than other alternatives. And for that, we probably would have needed to start several years ago – a topic on rivers here, on the atmosphere there, on pollution later still. If we had thought hard about the journey children would need to take in order for the concept of sustainable energy generation to make sense to them, then we would have been involved in curricular thinking. (Christine Counsell talks in her chapter about the proximal role some content has in preparing children to understand what is to come later.) But nobody was talking about that yet. Or if they were, I didn't realise that I needed to listen. I, like the children, didn't know what I didn't know.

Nor did I realise that around this time the three godfathers of the curriculum – Michael Young, E.D. Hirsch, and Daniel Willingham – were writing convincingly about curriculum, about why the *what* matters. Their reasons and emphases differed; arguments are not completely interchangeable and there are enduring disagreements between them (some of which Young mentions in his introductory chapter). There is common ground, however, in emphasizing that *what* we choose to teach in our schools is of vital significance. Once I discovered (via Twitter) Joe Kirby, Kris Boulton, Stuart Lock and Katharine Birbalsingh talking about the role of these godfathers, once I understood that knowledge is essential in enabling us to think critically and creatively, then a whole new world opened up. Here was the wonderful world of curriculum thinking.

The influence of all three of these godfathers is clear in all of the chapters in this book; though of the three, Michael Young's influence is the most marked, not least because he writes the opening chapter. In this chapter, Young shares various possibilities and pitfalls he has encountered as the concept of powerful knowledge he wrote about with David Lambert has begun to influence educational practice. (Young and Lambert, 2014). In subsequent chapters (and with no clever editorial planning on my part!) these various ideas are addressed by contributors. Young's concept is a fruitful one; even though none of the contributors had seen what he wrote in his chapter, they, in their various ways, have taken the concept of powerful knowledge into their workplaces and put it to work, realising and extending its possibilities and either overcoming potential pitfalls or showing that they weren't really pitfalls in the first place.

In expanding upon the idea of powerful knowledge, Young explains that:

- There is 'better knowledge' in different fields that we refer to as 'powerful knowledge'. It acquires its authority from the specialist communities of researchers in each discipline.
- All students, not just those identified as having 'academic ability', have the right to acquire this knowledge during their schooling.
- This 'better' or 'powerful' knowledge is specialised and takes the form of academic subjects.
- It is the basis of a curriculum that aims to be consistent with the disciplines where new knowledge is produced in the universities and research institutes.

In chapter 2, Ruth Ashbee expands upon this idea, using the work of sociologist of education Basil Bernstein to explain how school subjects relate to, yet differ from, academic and practitioner communities and to emphasize the vital role of disciplinary knowledge in ensuring that students are 'in the know' about the status of the knowledge they are learning. The legitimate question of whose knowledge we are teaching is answered by ensuring that disciplinary knowledge is taught alongside substantive knowledge. She suggests we explore what kind of things carry meaning in each of the different disciplines and asks how new knowledge is generated and contested.

In chapter 3, Aurora Reid discusses the idea that there might be 'better knowledge' that all students have the right to acquire. Is this cultural elitism? Is it patronising to think that certain cultural forms are just too hard for a particular kind of disadvantaged student and that they could not possibility understand or care about classical music or literature? Isn't it rather naive to think that if these students do not learn certain culturally significant content, they will be disadvantaged in terms of their ability to access wider cultural discourses?

Sonia Thompson, in chapter 4, shows what is possible in this regard. Working in a very deprived part of Birmingham, she and her school follow a curriculum that is unapologetically ambitious in in its scope and the children rise magnificently to the challenge. (I thought I had ambitious standards until I saw her year 6 children confidently contrasting the idea of the heroic in Friedrich Nietzsche with that in the work of Thomas Carlyle.) Alongside this, Sonia writes about respecting and learning from the home cultures of the children, using Luis Moll's concept of 'funds of knowledge', which can also be powerful.

One of the potential pitfalls Young is worried about is that an emphasis on cognitive science might lead teachers to over-focus on memorisation to the detriment of students developing a relationship with the knowledge they are learning. I would argue here with his understanding of Willingham's work; and in chapter 5, Neil Almond uses Willingham's work to show how students need to make the journey from shallower to deeper learning, the kind that enables the student to ask their own questions. A coherent curriculum is one that enables this journey. Young is worried that teachers might be under all sorts of constraints that leave them unable to develop a curriculum-led pedagogy that enables critical thinking. In chapter 6, Andrew Percival showcases the teacher as curriculum maker. By carefully identifying which knowledge is needed and then teaching that first, the power of the student to think critically and creatively is set free. The potential pitfall of cognitive science is not actually a pitfall at all, but an incredibly useful resource for putting knowledge to work in powerful, meaningful ways.

In chapter 7, Doug Lemov and Emily Badillo address another of Young's worries: the rise of scripted lessons, 'prepared by senior teachers independently of those in classrooms'. Before they started their English curriculum project, Lemov and Badillo probably would have feared them too, worrying that scripted lessons would undermine teachers' feelings of autonomy and professionalism. Their project sought to encourage teachers to incorporate background knowledge into their lessons. Disappointingly, the harsh realities of workload meant that this incorporation just didn't happen. Teachers did not have enough time to develop lesson plans with the level of detail necessary for their knowledge-rich approach. So, much to their surprise, they ended up developing a series of lessons for teachers to use. The real 'script' in their lessons is whatever text the class are currently studying, along with a plan. By using this plan, with previously thought-out questions and readily available non-fiction texts with relevant background knowledge, the teacher is freed to *prepare* the lesson rather than having to *plan* it from scratch. As a result, the students are enabled to understand and enjoy much more ambitious texts that previously.

Perhaps Young's biggest concern is how teachers can help all students, including those for whom academic endeavour is more hard won, benefit from a knowledge-rich approach. Lemov and Badillo show (as do Thompson, Almond and Percival) that if teachers think really carefully about the sequence of knowledge they teach, then students are capable of far more than we might have previously assumed. If we have not prepared the ground for complex concepts through introducing essential prerequisites beforehand, then we should not be surprised when students cannot make sense of them.

In chapter 8, Christine Counsell talks about the *proximal* role some content has in making the next bit of content understandable or some later accomplishment more secure. Subject matter is 'as hard or easy, as boring or interesting, as *prior encounter unlocks* [my emphasis]. To treat the curriculum as the progression model is to think about what effect each element may have on the pupil so that prior content joins new content to make new comparison accessible or fascinating.'

When teachers are skilled curriculum makers, the sequence of each element is carefully planned so as to unlock and render accessible and interesting even the most complex and ambitious of content. Counsell's chapter explains how senior leaders can ask questions of middle leaders to explore the extent to which the shape of the curriculum unlocks or impedes further learning.

Suggested route map through the book

Looking for practical guidance via case studies?	Want to explore questions of 'whose knowledge?'?	Want to understand the theory behind curriculum development?
Read	Read	Read
▼	▼	▼
Sonia Thompson, chapter 4 Neil Almond, chapter 5 Andrew Percival, chapter 6 Doug Lemov and Emily Badillo, chapter 7 Christine Counsell, chapter 8	Michael Young, chapter 1 Ruth Ashbee, chapter 2 Aurora Reid, chapter 3 Sonia Thompson, chapter 4	Michael Young, chapter 1 Ruth Ashbee, chapter 2 Christine Counsell, chapter 8

References

Young, M. and Lambert, D. (2014) *Knowledge and the future school*. London: Bloomsbury.

Author bio-sketch:

Clare Sealy has spent 30 years as a primary school teacher, 22 of them as head of St Matthias Primary School in Tower Hamlets in the East End of London. She has recently left headship to become head of curriculum and standards for the States of Guernsey. She blogs about how her school put educational research findings into practice at www.primarytimery. com. Her particular interests are the application of cognitive science in the classroom, rethinking assessment for learning and curriculum development. In 2018, she was named by *Tes* as one of the top ten most influential people in education.

FROM POWERFUL KNOWLEDGE TO THE POWERS OF KNOWLEDGE

PROFESSOR MICHAEL YOUNG

Introduction

My starting point is that schools in a democracy should all be working towards access to powerful knowledge for all their pupils. However, I want to raise some questions about the concept and how it has been used by schools. They reflect both theoretical criticisms and the experiences that schools have had in treating such access as a curriculum principle. This chapter builds on and extends an earlier paper (Young, 2018) and a paper by Christine Counsell in the same issue of *Impact* (Counsell, 2018).

Ten years ago, I contrasted the concept 'powerful knowledge' (PK) with the related concept 'knowledge of the powerful' (KOP) (Young, 2011). My aim in pairing them was to point to the important research priorities that the former concept suggested and my intended readership was my fellow researchers as well as those working in schools. The two concepts offered competing approaches to the question of social justice in education. KOP emphasised how the existing curriculum served the interests of those with power in society. It was in line with most sociology on the question of power in posing the question 'Who decides?' and 'In whose interests is the existing curriculum?' As Pierre Bourdieu put it, this treats the curriculum as 'an arbitrary selection of the culture supported by arbitrary powers'. In contrast, PK focuses on 'What knowledge?' It argues that there is knowledge – **powerful knowledge** – that is the best knowledge we have in each subject but that at least 50% of pupils in this country are denied access to.

However, this idea, especially the extent to which it mirrors the existing academic curriculum of GCSEs and A levels, is found in most selective and fee-paying public schools. It was, not surprisingly, picked up (in substance, although not initially in name) by right-wing think tanks such as Civitas and later by the Conservative-led coalition government in their 2011 *Framework for the National Curriculum* report. The coalition government used the concept primarily to criticise and distance themselves from the curriculum policies of the former Labour governments which had emphasised the experience of students rather than the knowledge that they acquired and focused on widening participation to make access easier for disadvantaged pupils.

As a result of government policies such as the EBacc, a version of PK became the benchmark for ranking schools and was adopted as a curriculum principle by many academies and free schools. At the same time, the government abolished hundreds of qualifications that did not fit their academic model. They were much influenced by the American E.D. Hirsch (Hirsch, 1988), and the think tank Civitas. So the roots of a more knowledge-led curriculum were far more on the political right than on the political left. The focus on knowledge and the support for a subject knowledge as the basis of the curriculum was heavily criticised by some on the left, despite the attempt by a small group of educational researchers – such as my colleague David Lambert and me (Young and Lambert, 2014) – who argued that a curriculum based on access to subject knowledge was in the long term the basis for a curriculum for all, and the only basis for overcoming our current educational inequalities.

Whereas the Conservative policies called for a return to a traditional view of the curriculum associated with academic subjects and accepted its association with inequalities, we argued that an emphasis on academic subjects – for all students – and the knowledge it made accessible was a left-wing issue concerned with social justice. At the same time, we failed to be explicit about the difficulties that schools adopting such an approach would inevitably face.

In my almost 50 years in educational research, I have never experienced another such controversial issue in education. I found myself criticised by long-standing friends and colleagues; one suggested that I, a lifelong Labour voter, must be one of Michael Gove's speechwriters. For the first time in my career, the divisions on a key educational issue were not just between left and right (as in the ongoing debate about comprehensive schools and selection) but within the left, about the nature of education itself. Are the basic questions in education about its distribution or about what is being distributed? And if the answer is the latter, how are they resolved? As Counsell puts it (much more elegantly), the basic questions we should be asking are questions about the knowledge of the methods of disciplines like history and physics and knowledge of the substantive knowledge of each.

What does 'powerful knowledge mean?

Powerful knowledge is an attempt to answer the above questions. It is worth spelling out the main features of the concept that are reflected in the book that David Lambert and I (Young and Lambert, 2014) wrote. They will not be unfamiliar:

20

- There is 'better knowledge' in different fields that we refer to as 'powerful knowledge'. It acquires its authority from the specialist communities of researchers in each discipline.
- All students, not just those identified as having 'academic ability', have the right to acquire this knowledge during their schooling.
- This 'better' or 'powerful' knowledge is specialised and takes the form of academic subjects.
- It is the basis of a curriculum that aims to be consistent with the disciplines where new knowledge is produced in the universities and research institutes.

We went on to make some arguments about the structure of this knowledge:

- First, that it emphasises two kinds of boundaries:
    o Those between subjects within the curriculum
    o Those between subject-based knowledge of the curriculum and the everyday knowledge that all children acquire through the experience of growing up

For teachers, this everyday knowledge of pupils is not to be dismissed; it is a resource they rely on, but it is not part of a curriculum that represents their aims as members of a profession. These boundaries are often experienced as alienating by pupils. However, although we accept this, we view these boundaries as potentially important structures through which students build their identities as learners and become 'acquirers of knowledge'. Overcoming this alienation of some pupils is a major difficulty that some pupils and their teachers face. It lies at the heart of some teachers' resistance to the idea of a knowledge-rich curriculum for all, and is an issue much neglected by educational researchers.

- Second, that, unlike the knowledge that students acquire spontaneously as they grow up, 'powerful knowledge' has to be acquired voluntarily by students at school. This means that unlike common sense or everyday knowledge, the 'powerful knowledge' that pupils attend school to acquire relies not on their experience but on the specialist knowledge of teachers.

To varying degrees, which largely reflect differences in the experiences of pupils outside school, the differences between everyday and subject knowledge represent a rupture between school and family life for pupils. It is this rupturing between school and non-school knowledge that has three consequences:

1. It poses the pedagogic problems that all teachers face.
2. It explains why, historically, some pupils become labelled 'less able' or low ability, and it is deemed appropriate for them not to follow a knowledge-rich curriculum.
3. It also explains why teaching is not, as the former Secretary of State Michael Gove once claimed, 'a craft for graduates that can be learned on the job'.

Like any profession, teachers need specialist professional knowledge to solve the complex problems they face. However, many current initiatives in teacher education such as Teach First and School Direct treat future teachers more like apprentices, not as future members of a profession. In my view these developments may expand the recruitment of teachers but are unlikely to lead to a higher quality teaching profession and almost certainly will not lead to a curriculum that is more knowledge-based.

Powerful knowledge in practice

The knowledge-led curriculum is a radical ideal which relies as much on a vision of a future more equal society as on improvements in the schools or better educational research. As with any vision, it raises problems in practice. For example:

- In emphasising 'knowledge content', it places a strong priority on achieving measurable outcomes, and little on the process of achieving these outcomes.
- It is difficult for schools under pressure for results to resist the metaphor of 'knowledge transmission' and recognise that, with its passive model of the learner, it has severe limitations.

A common claim by principals of some academies and free schools is that 'we teach knowledge'. However, this seems to portray acquiring knowledge as being like an injection that is mechanically inserted into the minds of pupils. Or, to change the metaphor, that knowledge is absorbed into pupil brains like typing text into a computer. The influence of computing on the models of learning generated by cognitive science is not hard to see. Pupils' brains are often treated as easily predictable, programmable and insular, like computers. In reality, of course, we have little direct access to them. How knowledge is assimilated by pupils is influenced by many factors, including their social interactions with teachers and fellow pupils in school and parents and friends at home.

Any teacher wants their pupils to acquire a relationship with knowledge like their own. However, teaching viewed as as the transmission of knowledge excludes the process by which students develop a relationship with knowledge. It treats the knowledge that makes up the curriculum of a subject as inert – more like the way a computer treats information. Absorbing inert bits of information is at best memorisation. The only capacity it can ensure is that the bits of information can be 'reproduced' in tests.

Ideally, a knowledge-led curriculum should treat school subjects not just as bodies of knowledge but as communities of teachers and researchers and pupils as neophyte members of such communities. All too frequently, a knowledge-rich curriculum can lead to an emphasis on memorisation, what charter schools in the USA describe as 'zero-tolerance discipline', and (in extreme cases) to scripted lessons prepared by senior teachers independently of those in classrooms.

These trends I have referred to are not caused by the new emphasis on knowledge in education or by the intentions of schools adopting a knowledge-led curriculum. They have two kinds of causes. One is professional and can be overcome or at least minimised by appropriate research in collaboration with teachers. However, there are also external causes of the knowledge-led curriculum becoming associated with a focus on memorisation. Two examples are worth highlighting. First is the low value placed on teaching as a profession in this country; and second is the uneven distribution of resources among schools, both within the public sector and between the public and private sectors.

It is my view that the most positive outcome of the last decade of curriculum reforms, regardless of its actual achievements, is the idea that 'access to knowledge for all' is the primary purpose of schooling. It contrasts strongly with two older progressive reforms: the 1944 Education Act which promised 'secondary education for all' and established the tripartite system of secondary schooling; and the 1965 policy of the Labour government (promising 'comprehensive schools for all') which phased out most selection at 11. Neither challenged the tripartite curriculum structure between academic, technical and modern; both accepted that a knowledge-rich curriculum was only appropriate for a limited (albeit growing) section of each cohort. A curriculum based on 'powerful knowledge for all' was only intended for some by the government that introduced it, and it was just too radical for many in the education community without an equally radical change in society. For those of us who proposed and believed in at least the possibility of powerful knowledge for all, we failed in two ways. The first failure was a lack of honesty in communicating about what was achievable within the present system; the second was being explicit about the kind of wider social changes we envisaged as being necessary for more wide-ranging educational change. The next section discusses some further issues concerned with the practical implementation of a knowledge-rich curriculum.

Powerful knowledge in practice; further issues

In this section I want to consider how the concept of powerful knowledge has been used, sometimes explicitly, often implicitly, by researchers, government and some of those in schools, and comment on some of the criticisms that have been made of it and some potential alternative ways of thinking.

I suggest three problems have arisen with the concept:

- *The ambiguous meaning of power*
- *The incompleteness of the model of powerful knowledge as a curriculum principle*
- *The neglect of the interdependence of curriculum and pedagogy*

The ambiguous meaning of power

In everyday speech, we talk about power to mean two different things – having 'power over' others and having the 'power to' think or act in new ways.

An example of having 'power over' something is how in education the curriculum can be seen as dominating pupils and limiting their freedom. A reaction against this has led to movements for creating curricula that emphasise children as creators of their own meanings and playing down the instructional role of the teacher. The idea of 'power to' reminds us of educational thinkers like the Brazilian Paulo Freire and the idea of education as emancipation. This also can place almost too much responsibility on the learner and give no role to the teacher. It is not surprising that student teachers can become confused by these contradictions – especially when power is linked to knowledge. The fundamental weakness of such an approach is that it does not fulfil its promises to teachers. Teachers on their own are not powerful; they acquire power as members of a profession and a union and in collaboration with governments, not independently of them. At best, the contradictory nature of power highlights the political nature of education – not political primarily in a 'choice of party' sense, but in the sense that education is always about the view a society has of itself.

The incompleteness of the model of powerful knowledge as a curriculum principle

Since David Lambert and I wrote the book *Knowledge and the Future School*, I have come to realise that there are two ways in which our concept of a curriculum was inadequate and perhaps why, in the blogs and Twitter comments, my name is often linked mistakenly with the American E.D. Hirsch – especially his early and most well-known book, subtitled 'What every American needs to know'.

Like Hirsch's idea of cultural literacy, though not explicitly, powerful knowledge focuses on lists of concepts and a subject structure with clear boundaries between the subjects. These are sequenced to guide learner progress.

These are important elements of a curriculum, but they mask another feature any model of curriculum needs to take account of: the extent to which a knowledge-based curriculum is a high-resource curriculum, especially (but not only) in relation to human resources. Curriculum subjects, as I explained in an earlier section, are not only sets of concepts and methods of enquiry; they are 'communities of specialists' who share ideas and values with specialists in other schools, with disciplinary specialists in universities and increasingly, internationally. They meet at conferences and publish in journals as ways of collectively evaluating ideas and improving what their subject can offer. This means that learning a subject successfully is not unlike joining a community initially as a beginner or neophyte and gradually developing new relationships and acquiring new knowledge. It means that teachers need to have not only a reliable store of subject knowledge, but also an understanding of their role as members of a virtual community of specialists which guarantees the knowledge they have.

Perhaps the most important point that follows is that if a school lacks the funds to employ qualified specialist teachers, it will be unable to claim to have a knowledge-based curriculum as more than something on paper; I know of a school where physics had to be taught by a teacher with a physical education degree.

Resources on which a knowledge-based curriculum depends also extend to specialist accommodation, like studios and workshops and specialist land facilities for sports – and of course the support that schools with a high proportion of middle-class pupils take for granted. These points may appear obvious, but when considering the annual GCSE and A levels, the ranking of schools is as much an expression of inequalities of per pupil funding and the private/state divide as it is evidence of the ability of pupils.

The neglect of the interdependence of curriculum and pedagogy

This is a point that applies to our book *Knowledge and the Future School* (Young and Lambert, 2014) – except for the chapter by David Lambert. He stresses the important idea that even though a curriculum may be laid down by exam syllabuses, teachers still have to 'make' the curriculum with their students – they are 'curriculum makers'. However, while this is an important point, its danger is that it can leave the 'curriculum making' to teachers, and does not emphasise enough the constraints they are under. We need, I think, a model of curriculum making that incorporates how teachers might engage with these constraints.

While it is important for a school to stipulate the knowledge in its curriculum, on its own, it can leave knowledge as more like information and the curriculum as little more than a store of codified knowledge. The knowledge in a curriculum can remain inert until, as I argued earlier, it becomes part of sets of relations – between groups of teachers, and between teachers and their students as neophyte specialists acquiring and making sense of sequences of subject concepts in different ways.

Cognitive scientists such as Daniel Willingham have become popular among those who write about teaching (some of whom are teachers). They emphasise the importance of acquiring and memorising bodies of subject knowledge for later use. However, a focus on memorisation does not necessarily encourage students to develop a 'relationship to knowledge' that leads to new questions. For understandable reasons, a school adopting a knowledge-led curriculum can spend too much time on testing whether students have memorised the knowledge of previous years. The difficult twin task for teachers (whose pupils inevitably have a diversity of learning needs) is how to base the curriculum on pedagogised knowledge and how to develop a curriculum-led pedagogy. This is not to discourage memorisation, which is an integral part of any successful learning, but to insist that it is not an end in itself – students need to learn that memorisation is a step to acquiring new knowledge.

Responding to the critics of powerful knowledge

The arguments against a curriculum based on 'powerful knowledge for all' have been of two kinds.

The first are the left-wing, anti-racist and feminist thinkers who see 'powerful knowledge' as another way of imposing an alien culture on those who are assumed to have either no culture of their own or the wrong culture. My response to these criticisms is not that they should be dismissed – they highlight the major inequalities of our society. It is that their criticism becomes criticism for its own sake. They point to the limitations of any attempt to shift the unequal distribution of knowledge through the curriculum but offer no alternatives except radical changes that are always on the next horizon.

The second group of critics need to be taken more seriously. I am referring to the teachers – usually but not necessarily older teachers – who draw on their experience and doubt whether a 'powerful knowledge'-based curriculum can be successful with a significant section of slow or disaffected learners who appear to lack both motivation and ability. As an example, I remember a head opposed to the EBacc whose comment was that his school did not have the kind of pupils who would be able to study economics or physics.

My response is that pupils' acquisition of knowledge at school is only partly the responsibility of teachers. Education takes place in a particular society in which knowledge is distributed unequally, and this shapes what schools can do. Whether schools can achieve more is always a political question as well as a pedagogic one. When I went to university, only 3% of my cohort did so; few would have predicted that 50 or more years later it would be 50% of each cohort. In some Nordic countries, the figure is nearer to 100% – but of course they have more much egalitarian societies in general.

Increase in participation in higher education is not primarily a consequence of dramatic changes in the curriculum or pedagogy, though they have changed – the whole society has changed and is changing. However, it is still a society based on systematic and apparently difficult-to-overcome inequalities. This, as I touched on earlier, is a political (not just an educational) question, although any political change that does not include educational changes will face similar problems to those we face today.

Some conclusions

Powerful knowledge is not a tool that can tell you what knowledge to include in your classes or how to structure them – that is your responsibility as members of the teaching profession. It is not a curriculum principle in precise terms or the basis of short-term goals or outcomes that can be unambiguously measured. However – and this is not easy to express – it is an approach to the curriculum that recognises that the way in which teachers relate to pupils and the tasks a teacher encourages their pupils to undertake may be as important as what is stipulated in a school's curriculum.

Concluding this chapter has reminded me that acquiring real knowledge is hard, slow, incremental work, whether I am trying to help one of my doctoral students make sense of Vygotsky or Bernstein or a science teacher is helping their class of 13-year-olds understand valency (as I used to try to do as a chemistry teacher).

In our book, David Lambert and I proposed that 'powerful knowledge for all' should be a curriculum principle for all schools. Despite the criticisms I now accept, it is still an educational principle I endorse. However, as a short-term goal, it can be unhelpfully unrealistic. We need to remember the scale of our task – that somehow we want the knowledge stored in the collective minds of the teaching profession and expressed in the curriculum to become (after 10 or 12 years) present in the minds of all students. We know this happens in individual cases but not yet for the majority. Finding ways of increasing the numbers of those for whom this is a reality is a radical aim, and it is not easy to make real progress. However, it is nothing more than making our education system democratic – and that is what we, as a society, claim to be.

References

Counsell, C. (2018) 'Taking curriculum seriously', *Impact* 4. Retrieved from www.bit.ly/38MXnZJ

Hirsch, E. D. (1988) *Cultural literacy: what every American needs to know.* New York, NY: Random House.

Young, M. (2011) 'The return to subjects: a sociological perspective on the UK coalition government's approach to the 14–19 curriculum', *The Curriculum Journal* 22 (2) pp. 265–278.

Young, M. (2018) 'A knowledge-led curriculum: possibilities and pitfalls', *Impact* 4. Retrieved from: www.bit.ly/2wPyf7A

Young, M. and Lambert, D. (2014) *Knowledge and the future school.* London: Bloomsbury.

Note: I am only including a very small group of references. Any reader who wants to raise any questions or wants further references that relate to the issues this chapter refers to is very welcome to email me: michael.young@ucl.ac.uk

Author bio-sketch:

Michael Young studied natural sciences at Cambridge University and, after one year with Shell Chemical Company, became a secondary school science teacher in south London. After completing a BSc in Sociology through part-time study, he studied for an MA in Sociology at the University of Essex with an ESRC studentship and was appointed lecturer (and later senior lecturer) in sociology of education at the Institute of Education, UCL. In 1986, he founded and led the Institute's post-16 education centre and with Ken Spours launched the first MA in Vocational Education and Training in the UK. His specialist field of research became the role of vocational qualifications and national qualification frameworks and took him to many different countries, including Brazil and South Africa and visiting professorships in English, South African, and Chinese universities. The Chinese translation of his 2007 book Bringing Knowledge Back In was recently published in Beijing.

More recently, he has returned to his original interest in the secondary school curriculum. This led to a close collaboration and several articles and books with Johan Muller (University of Cape Town) and the book *Knowledge and the Future School* that Michael wrote with his colleague David Lambert. In his current work, he has continued his long-term interest in extending access to knowledge in schools and remains a part-time professor of sociology of curriculum at UCL's Institute of Education.

WHY IT'S SO IMPORTANT TO UNDERSTAND SCHOOL SUBJECTS – AND HOW WE MIGHT BEGIN TO DO SO

RUTH ASHBEE

Making meaning is a uniquely human behaviour. Visual representations, abstract concepts, universal laws, metaphors, narratives, and jokes are all things that we and only we do. The sociological structures that allow us to make meaning to the extent and depth that we do are the subject disciplines: science, mathematics, literature, history, art, and so on. In schools, we teach the cousins of these disciplines: the school subjects. The job of schools is therefore to teach children about meaning – about what it means to be human. This is a significant responsibility and carries with it moral imperatives: we are compelled to strive to do this job as well as we possibly can.

It is vital that educators seek to understand the nature of the disciplines and the school subjects. This knowledge should inform discussions and decisions around both curriculum and pedagogy within schools, and should also feed into an informed broader discourse around curricula in schools and their relations with the subject disciplines. If we believe that all children are entitled to a good education, then decisions around both what constitutes a good education and how best to make it a reality must be informed by an understanding of the subject disciplines which rightly sit at the heart of the school curriculum model. What's more, these issues lie at the heart of democracy and a free society.

The subject disciplines make different types of meaning, and they make it in different ways. It is for this reason that we have different subject disciplines at all, and not just one big subject. The knowledge in the different disciplines is about different things, and so it has different properties and is produced through different processes. These differences are important, and we should study them.

School subjects come from the subject disciplines, but they are not just smaller versions of them. Sociologist of education Basil Bernstein pointed out that in school subjects, knowledge has been recontextualised from the subject discipline:

(Bernstein, 1990)

In school subjects, students do not just begin learning the body of knowledge that exists in the discipline, starting in one small corner from which they will steadily progress through the rest of the knowledge as they continue their education. In the field of recontextualisation, the domain of the professionals who write things like the national curriculum and school textbooks, decisions are made about what will be best to include in the school subject. There might be fundamentals that need to be mastered before later study, or core knowledge around which new knowledge can meaningfully be built. In addition, since most children will not continue the study of any one particular subject, and because the purpose of education is not solely or even mainly to prepare students for later study, the questions must be asked: 'What is the best knowledge for children to leave school with should they discontinue their study in this subject?'; 'What is the most important knowledge for citizens?'; 'Which knowledge will bring the most meaning?'

It is important for educators to understand the existence and importance of recontextualisation. It is important because, cognitively, knowledge that is just copied and pasted from the academic field will not be accessible to children – it needs to be put into an appropriate form so that the journey can be successfully begun and developed. It is also important because the amount of knowledge in any discipline is just so vast, and since most children will finish their study of most subjects at age 16, we must make sure that the knowledge they do learn has been chosen for its value, rather than just being all the knowledge from the first corner of the academic discipline, whatever that may be. If you visit a city, you want to visit all the key points of interest, not just the street on which you enter the city. Furthermore, pedagogical mistakes have been made in the past as a result of not understanding the existence and importance of recontextualisation. An over-emphasis on investigative work in mathematics, for example, before basic knowledge has been mastered, has often been justified because 'this is how mathematicians work'. The fact that people in the academic discipline work in a particular way doesn't necessarily mean it's the best way for children to work in the earlier stages of their education.

Equally, we must be critical of recontextualisation and engage in discourse that explores and questions the details. All editing is an exercise of power, and those exercising this power must be held to account. Is it right that students should learn something false (such as a simplified model in science) in order to facilitate understanding later on? In science, there is broad agreement that the falsehood of electron shells is a useful fiction and performs a virtuous role in the education of children in science – but acceptance of things like this must be the outcome of a critical discourse and not simply done by either educators or academics without question. Recontextualisation involves choice and inclusion, giving rise to the question of 'Whose knowledge?' – and changes to curriculum such as the inclusion of texts by writers from other cultures are the direct result of critical discourse around recontextualisation. This conversation is a healthy one and must be continued as part of a democratic society.

Education is ultimately a moral activity. We must educate children because they are entitled to knowledge and to prepare them for further study, should they pursue it. The content of that education must be recontextualised in order to a) make it cognitively appropriate and b) ensure that the breadth of the education is optimised, since most children will not continue the subject beyond school. And all of the decisions that are made around this knowledge must be subject to checks from both the academic and education communities, who have a responsibility to engage with the discourse, to understand it and to contribute to it.

This discourse is better informed by an understanding of the knowledge natures and structures in the disciplines and school subjects. We can ask two broad questions of a discipline: 'What meaning does it make?' and 'How is this meaning made?' This gives us our two categories of knowledge: substantive and disciplinary, respectively.

It is vital that we understand the nature of substantive and disciplinary knowledge in our subjects. Students are entitled to learn wonderful substantive knowledge because it is their inheritance. This is perhaps best expressed in the following quote from Robert Tressell's *The Ragged-Trousered Philanthropists*:

> What we call civilisation – the accumulation of knowledge which has come down to us from our forefathers – is the fruit of thousands of years of human thought and toil. It is not the result of the labour of the ancestors of any separate class of people who exist today, and therefore it is by right the common heritage of all. (Tressell, 1914)

Substantive knowledge allows children to find meaning in the world.

The teaching of disciplinary knowledge is vital for three reasons.

Firstly, the creation of any curriculum is an exercise of power (Counsell, 2018). This matters more for some subjects than others, and it causes more arguments for some subjects than for others. The fact that is impossible to teach, for example, all of history, and that there are no universally agreed criteria for choosing what to include and what to exclude (as there arguably are in science and mathematics, for example) means that the choice of periods, areas and interpretations studied is unavoidably and necessarily laden with personal and/or political preference, and that there will never be a complete consensus on what should be included. Without disciplinary knowledge, this choice and exclusion arrangement could be both misleading and potentially sinister: if students leave school thinking 'This is all the history there is' then they have fallen foul of some kind of propaganda machine, either intentional or unintentional. If we can teach children that 'even the curriculum itself, as they received it, was one such selection, and must not be confused with the whole domain' (Counsell, 2018), then we will have given them an understanding of the limitations of curriculum and the breadth of the discipline. Students trained in disciplinary knowledge will be equipped to critically evaluate the inclusion of the knowledge in the curriculum they have studied, and to ask what else could have been included. Disciplinary knowledge, then, allows us to sit more comfortably within the 'Whose knowledge?' debate.

Secondly, teaching disciplinary knowledge opens up the codes of the different subjects that would otherwise remain hidden to students without an academic background. University-educated people tend to have (at least a degree of) understanding of the norms and behaviours of the different disciplines, and children of people from these backgrounds tend to absorb this understanding. To other children, the demarcation of subjects can remain a mystery – without dinner-table conversations on the similarities and differences between history and English literature, for example, children are left either to work these things out for themselves, with a high risk of developing misconceptions, or simply to never even think about these things.

Finally, as Clare Sealy points out (Sealy, 2019), ignorance of disciplinary codes and their respective claims to truths and normative claims, is a gift to totalitarian regimes. Propaganda makes rich use of blurred disciplinary boundaries, touting scientific 'facts' without evidence, and writing 'history' without sources. Thus in a free society, we must treasure and fiercely guard our knowledge of the disciplinary. Paradoxically, the best way to guard knowledge and prevent it being corrupted is to share it, to teach it, to put it into the curriculum.

How can we further our understanding of the nature of the substantive and disciplinary knowledge in our disciplines and school subjects? Traditional discussions around the subject disciplines have centred around the 'two cultures' characterisation of the arts and the sciences, but this does not get us very far. We need a more detailed and nuanced analysis to allow us to see the true nature of these discourses.

Drawing on work from curriculum and knowledge thinkers such as Karl Maton, Christine Counsell, Michael Fordham, and Richard Kueh, the following eight questions can be used to reach a greater understanding of disciplines and school subjects:

1. What is the quest of this discipline?
2. How many subjects actually is it?
3. What kinds of things carry meaning in the discipline?
4. How is new knowledge generated in the discipline's field of production?
5. How is the knowledge linked in the discipline?
6. What does it mean to practise this subject in a scholarly way in the classroom?
7. How does the recontextualised school subject differ from the discipline and what purposes do these differences serve?
8. What can and can't/should and shouldn't this subject do?

The insights from these questions allow a more productive discourse around recontextualisation and lead to better-informed discussions and decisions in schools around curriculum planning and teaching in the classroom.

Let us explore each of them in turn.

1. What is the quest of this discipline?

All subjects seek to do something – or rather the people engaging in them are seeking to do something, either collectively or individually. This quest may have changed over time or a single discipline may encompass more than one quest. In science, the quest is to explain and predict the behaviour of the natural world through fundamental principles by observing and testing the world in a controlled manner. In geography, the quest is to understand how the earth and its resources interact with large-scale human behaviours by drawing on ideas from various fields and applying them to geographical cases. In history, we seek to understand the past by weaving together the remnants left for us. In art, the quest is to create visual pieces, for beauty, expression, or both. In music, it is to create pieces in sound that are beautiful or evoke a particular emotion or experience. Understanding the quest of a discipline is vital to informing discussion of the recontextualisation, content, and pedagogy of a school subject.

2. How many subjects actually is it?

Very often the consideration of knowledge in a subject is made much more difficult than it needs to be by the fact that a single subject title obscures a diversity of subjects underneath. Richard Kueh, for example, has argued that religious studies actually encompasses theology, history, philosophy and ethics (Kueh, 2017). Geography has a similarly composite nature, whereas history and mathematics are relatively 'pure'. This is not a value judgement though – the more composite subjects allow us to teach things that must be understood in breadth and diversity of knowledge. Understanding them as composites or as multi-stranded, however, allows us to see the structures in each strand, rather than coming up against a wall when some areas of knowledge behave differently to other areas. This in turn allows us to think about what should be included in a subject's curriculum, to sequence the knowledge in the curriculum effectively, and to be more intentional about pedagogy.

3. What kinds of things carry meaning in the discipline?

In some subjects, such as science and geography, there are ideas which, although discovered or created by individuals, transcend the individuals and can be taught independently of them and their original works. In other subjects, the works themselves carry the meaning – in art, literature and music, it is the pieces themselves that are important. The answers to this question can inform discussion of what the objects of study in a school curriculum should be: students need to study Newton's laws but not the *Principia* itself, whereas they do need to study the works of Picasso himself, and not just the ideas in those works.

4. How is new knowledge generated in the discipline's field of production?

Many but not all of the disciplines have their field of production located primarily in universities. What do practitioners do in their production of new knowledge? Do they experiment? Observe? Create? Explore? Write? And how is this knowledge approved by the subject community? Is entrance into the received body of knowledge unlocked through peer review? Re-creation of experiment? Checking of figures? Critical acclaim? Laying out these 'codes' explicitly allows intentional planning for disciplinary knowledge in the curriculum. In science, for example, we teach about control variables and peer review, and in geography we teach about sampling. Even in art, the practice of holding a viewing, for example of Year 11 final pieces, helps to induct students into the key role of exhibition in the approval of work in this field.

5. How is the knowledge linked in the discipline?

The knowledge given by a discipline – the meaning it makes – can be thought of as existing in a web of interconnected pieces. The number and organisation of these connections is a key feature of the nature of the discipline and its object(s) of study. In science, the knowledge is highly linked and highly organised in what Bernstein termed a vertical structure: a few underlying principles explain a large number of things. In geography, the structure is much less vertical in that although there are many principles, they do not follow a hierarchy in how fundamental they are. There are many links within the knowledge in that a geographical question may involve knowledge of landscape, resources, climate, population, migration and economics – but there is little ascendance in terms of less to more fundamental in these components. Technology has a similar 'horizontal but highly linked' structure, as does art, while mathematics has a very vertical structure, with many links within branches and few between. Being able to see these links allows careful sequencing of knowledge in a curriculum in order to allow students to travel a meaningful journey along the curriculum path. It allows us to see where additional knowledge should be added in to the curriculum in order to join sections of the web and make the meaning therein available to students. Thus, for example, while the geographical proximity of the origins of Judaism, Christianity and Islam may not be specified in the local agreement curriculum, we might add it since it helps join the web to explore similarities in the religions and their relationships to each other over time.

6. What does it mean to practise this subject in a scholarly way in the classroom?

The necessity of recontextualisation means that practice in the classroom will often or even always be different from practice in the field of production. This does not mean, though, that 'anything goes'. We must ask what it means to practise the subject in the most scholarly way – scholarly meaning 'faithful to the subject discipline'. People will of course bring different starting points to their interpretations in answer to this question, and it will be natural to not find consistent agreement. But the disagreements should be over what is the best thing in relation to the true nature of the discipline and its effective recontextualisation; an informed discussion rather than an ideological war. We should be asking questions like 'Does creating a newspaper report on the Battle of Hastings have a place in the scholarly history classroom? Does retrieval practice of vocabulary have a place in the scholarly art classroom? How much time should be spent on practising explanations in the scholarly science classroom?' A focus on both the nature of the discipline and the role of recontextualisation will create the conditions for good quality discussion on curricular and pedagogical matters within school subjects.

7. How does the recontextualised school subject differ from the discipline and what purposes do these differences serve?

Following question 6 above, it is useful to lay out explicitly the ways in which the recontextualised school subject is different from the discipline in the field of production – and the ways in which they are similar. We might then come to ways in which we think they ought to be more similar or different, and feed this into the critical discourse. We might note that anatomy is present in the field of production of art but not in the school subject; and we might then ask if we think that it should be included. We might note that the knowledge in the school maths curriculum looks little like the knowledge used by mathematicians in their everyday work, and note that that is as it should be, due to the highly vertical and ascending nature of knowledge in mathematics. Knowledge of these reflections and departures enables not only the critical discourse but also intentional curriculum planning and the avoidance of pedagogical mistakes stemming from attempting to emulate the field of production at all times.

8. What can and can't/should and shouldn't the subject do?

It is useful to consider the boundary conditions of a subject in order to see its nature and scope more clearly. Science can give you a best bet for objective truth but it can't give you a value judgement. Geography can explain developments but it can seldom predict them with any accuracy. History can help us to understand the past but it can never give us a true, objective account of events, for such a thing does not exist. In history, we should avoid anachronism and projection; in religious studies, we should form opinions and justify them, while being aware of the legitimacy of other opinions. In science, we have no room for opinions; we have conclusions and we support them with data. These boundary conditions are useful when asking what should be included in a school subject curriculum; too often in the past, pedagogy has made use of activities which go against the codes and norms of the subject. These activities are a significant opportunity cost, as students are, for example, using up time writing letters to MPs to convince them about the need for wind turbines when they could be practising writing about the science of wind turbines and their context. Furthermore, doing these activities obscures the codes of the disciplines and keeps them hidden from students. Students leave school with a confused understanding of the nature, operation and scope of the disciplines, and this is problematic for the reasons discussed above.

The diversity of the subject disciplines, then, reflects the ambition of humanity in making meaning in many fields and in many ways. Education must follow this model, and keep the diversity and integrity of the subjects at its heart. We must teach the substantive knowledge because it brings forth meaning from the world; and we must teach the disciplinary knowledge because it delineates the subjects, it helps to circumvent the problem of 'Whose knowledge?', and because it should be a prized possession of a free society. The surest way to keep knowledge safe is to teach it and to teach it well.

Recontextualisation is key to the teaching of knowledge; copying and pasting from the disciplines into school curricula will not work. It should be continuously debated and evaluated, however, by informed members of the field of production (academics) and the field of reproduction (teachers).

We need to understand the nature of the knowledge in the disciplines and school subjects if we are to faithfully carry out our responsibility of teaching knowledge. By asking about the quests, diversity, meaning, generation of knowledge, links, scholarly classroom practice, recontextualisation and boundary conditions of disciplines and school subjects, we can begin to gain the understanding we need in order to fulfil our roles as teachers and academics in the pursuit of providing what we can truly call a good education – an education for good.

Acknowledgements

Without having referenced any particular works by any of the following people, discussion with them and interaction with their work has been of enormous help in developing the ideas expressed here: Karl Maton, Christine Counsell, Michael Young, Atlanta Plowden, Helen Georgiou, Michael Fordham, Matt Burnage, Richard Kueh, Tim Jenner, Ben Ranson, Ben Newmark, Pritesh Raichura.

References

Bernstein, B. (1990) *Class, codes and control, volume IV: the structuring of pedagogic discourse.* London: Routledge.

Counsell, C. (2018) 'Taking curriculum seriously', *Impact* 4. Retrieved from www.bit.ly/38MXnZJ

Kueh, R. (2017) 'Religious education and the "knowledge problem"' in Castelli, M. and Chater, M. (eds) *We need to talk about religious education.* London: Jessica Kingsley, pp. 53–70.

Sealy, C. (2019) 'A matter of fact?', *Tes*, 11 October.

Tressell, R. (1914) *The ragged-trousered philanthropists.* London: Grant Richards.

Author bio-sketch:

Ruth Ashbee is assistant headteacher for curriculum at the Telford Priory School. Having studied history and philosophy of science at University College London, Ruth went on to become a physics teacher, first in London and then Telford, before becoming lead practitioner prior to her current role. She is an editor at CogSciSci, the research-informed science subject association, and the author of Knowledge Quiz: Physics (John Catt). Ruth's blog (www.rosalindwalker.wordpress.com) is a source of physics booklets, science teaching, and general curriculum discussion.

CULTURAL CAPITAL, CRITICAL THEORY AND CURRICULUM

AURORA REID

The focus on cultural capital in the new (2019) English Ofsted framework has catapulted discussions of this once obscure sociological term into educational discourse. Whist many with a progressive bent welcome an approach that puts disadvantaged students front and centre and begins to consider the child more holistically (or at least recognises that a good set of exam results is not all a young person should leave school with), much has been noted of the roots of the term in Pierre Bourdieu's (1984) analysis of how power is reproduced through 'elite' cultural signifiers (Didau, 2019) – in particular, the irony of this term, which originated as a critique of the elite being used a tool or benchmark to ensure schools 'cement social conservativism' in a way that writes off the experiences of working-class students (Mansell, 2019) by essentially teaching them to 'pass' as middle class. Further, it raises questions of whose culture should be taught and to what ends: for the sheer joy of it; for personal growth; to support a UCAS application; to ensure one can converse comfortably with those in the higher echelons of power? These are questions which I believe are, in essence, political ones and ones which we should be grappling with; and yet the debate around them tends to shut down conversation rather than growing it.

The tensions around the term are, I believe, illuminated by a vignette about an (unnamed) academy sponsor and Conservative Party donor. In discussion with a colleague, he believed that the mark of an effective curriculum (both in the classroom and extracurricular) would be if a young person from the school were able to sit alongside him at a table, eat well and hold their own in a conversation with him. Whilst it is unfair to characterise this as his only goal for disadvantaged students, I think it does illustrate the thinking behind some of the decisions being made on the right of education. To my mind, it points to what could be termed a 'PPE approach' that sees the goal of knowledge acquisition as being able to successfully navigate a dinner party. Moreover, what about the experience for the young person sitting there? Would it be empowering or would there be a sense of alienation, of passing as something they felt they were not – or worse, being on show? There is plenty to critique in this approach.

Perhaps it is easy for those of us on the left to look on this perspective with disdain and to criticise the paternalism of the upper classes. However, a further reading also reveals a broader concern that many in education share: the desire for all our young people to be able to hold their own in circles of power and even have a seat at the proverbial table. I think a note of pragmatism is also important: for better or worse, this discourse (along with these people) has a hold in education, and we have another term (at least) of a Conservative government, so writing this view off is not an option.

In this chapter, I will touch on some of the thinking of the Frankfurt School, a group of critical theorists who explored the relationship between culture and power in the interwar years. I will do this in order to think about the term 'cultural capital' in a way that is constructively critical – that is, borrowing from ideas that might traditionally be seen as the preserve of the left or the right in a way that is both principled and pragmatic. Principled because I have no qualms about my politics; I believe that education has a radical goal: to disrupt the status quo and drive society towards equality. But pragmatic because, as those of us who work in schools in deprived areas (particularly in the inner cities) well know, if we want to see our disadvantaged young people have the best opportunities, it means (in part) they need to get into good universities and have access to a wide range of cultural experiences and choices. Not that this is a silver bullet for all of society's problems, but the reality of poverty, gangs and violence is what many of our young people will face if school does not offer them a vision of something different. In addition, we also know that five more years of austerity will further entrench this inequality and strip schools of their resources. In this time of scarcity, we need to look to what is in our power to control and what is worth fighting over.

We need to move beyond a framing of the debate, which sets out cultural capital as either a panacea that ensures social mobility (despite the broader context of austerity and inequality) or an elitist 'plot'. This plays into reified notions of left and the right that paralyse the conversation and, ultimately, harm rather than help the young people that I do believe we (who work in education) all set out to support. It divides us and prevents us focusing on what is within our power to change for our students.

Maybe this has been the case since time immemorial, but certainly since I joined teaching during the heights of Michel Gove's education reforms in England, the lines between left and right, amplified by Twitter and perhaps reflecting the post-Trump and -Brexit political mood more generally in the

UK, have become extremely polarised. The debate typically divides along key lines and for those firmly embedded in the 'Twittersphere', there are a number of markers that will be recognisable as a dog whistle for fierce and moralising debate.

On the one hand, there are those who think that education is improved by driving up academic standards, teaching the canon (the best that has been thought and said) from the front with unrelenting discipline, not making excuses for students and excluding (or isolating) them if need be. They see those who do not take this approach as lazy and institutionalised, not prepared to make the hard choices and sometimes be disliked by the children and their communities in order to do what's in their best interests. The opposing ideological standpoint sees this approach as patriarchal and disempowering; it recognises that the reasons for disadvantage and disengagement are complex and resolving them requires attending to the structures of inequality as well as culture, community and individual needs. There is often a hesitancy to impose punitive sanctions or to teach knowledge for fear of indoctrinating or alienating communities. It sees the roots of disadvantage as external to the individual or community – in structural racism and inequality or in the ills of capitalism. It seems to me that in these debates, people so often speak past each other. I wrote a blog post in 2018 (Reid, 2018) that was an attempt to start a conversation between these two perspectives and which suggested that those on the left should not isolate themselves from discussions about a knowledge-rich curriculum (or allow conservatives to have a monopoly on this conversation) for fear of returning to a Gradgrindian Victorian ethos. It is important to note that I am not the only voice making this point. In fact, these debates, which have recently become party political, have a long history in post-Marxist critical theory. I follow many eminent thinkers – including Michael Young, Christine Counsell and the many contributors to this book – in highlighting the compatibility of traditional methods and progressive aims. Some of these thinkers are turning to the hashtag #leftytrad to try to broaden the debate on Twitter.

The Frankfurt School explored notions of culture in Germany in the interwar years, with the intention to bring 19th-century Marxism into the 20th century. Theodor Adorno wrote *The Philosophy of Modern Music* in 1949. A polemic on popular music, it argued that 'pop' functioned as part of culture industry of capitalist society by imbuing its listener with a false consciousness that contributed to their domination. He argued that radical art and music alone preserve the 'untransfigured' truth of human suffering.

The elitism of this approach, which associated goodness with 'high culture' and false consciousness with 'mass culture', was criticised by Georg Lukacs, who argued in *The Theory of the Novel* (1971) that

> A considerable part of the leading German intelligentsia, including Adorno, have taken up residence in the Grand Hotel Abyss which I described ... as a beautiful hotel, equipped with every comfort, on the edge of an abyss, of nothingness, of absurdity.

This critique, which has a ring of the anti-intellectual 'metropolitan elite' refrain that conservatives have been drumming up for some time, recognises that left-wing academia can be detached from most peoples' realities and therefore seen as paternalistic. Like Lucas, Walter Benjamin (1969) was critical of Adorno's approach. He saw 'high culture' as the treasures of the bourgeoisie, blemished by the suffering of the poor. He located mass culture as a potential site of resistance through allowing audiences to participate and interact with art in new ways, not simply under the 'dominion' of the author.

These conflicting approaches speak to the heart of the issues around cultural capital. I believe it is in this tension, the place between the polarities, that some truth can be found. Adorno raises questions for us when planning our curriculum (in the broadest sense; I will talk more about extra-curricular later). What should be learnt? Do some subjects or forms have innately more value? To echo an old refrain, is Mozart more valuable for students to study than Stormzy? And what is meant by 'valuable'? Does that mean more conducive to radical thought, more likely to improve a young person's life chances or those of their community? Much has been discussed of Matthew Arnold's often quoted notion that the curriculum should comprise 'the best that has been thought and said', but what constitutes 'the best' is innately political and should rightly be contested.

However, whilst I recognise the concerns about elitisms and paternalism, I would argue that Adorno has a point: not that mass culture in itself lacks value but that there is freedom to be found in the high arts, and those treasures do not deserve to stay the preserve of the bourgeoisie. Why else is it that *Romeo and Juliet* speaks to conflicted and lovesick teenagers everywhere, or a piece of Bach has the capacity to move someone (totally illiterate in classical music) to tears? They offer something that is universal and perhaps liberatory.

That schools must take students outside of their own experience is a point of principle for me. Building on Michael Young's concept of powerful knowledge

(Young and Lambert, 2014), schools can help young people 'to envisage alternatives'. That is not to write off entire cultures or communities by insinuating that children need rescuing from them, but simply to acknowledge the reality that for many of the young people I work with, poverty, drugs, violence, social media and video games fill up a disproportionately large part of their lives. Therefore, we cannot be diverted by a notion of relevance which is guided solely by what the students already recognise. It is a lazy (and I would go as far as to say bigoted) argument to say we should teach the students about grime music because they could not possibility understand or care about classical music; and it is naive to think that if they do not learn the canon of literature then they will not be disadvantaged in terms of their ability to access wider cultural discourses.

However, to return to grime as the example, it is not to say that grime does not have value as an art form, or that it is not important that students see themselves and their communities mirrored in their curriculum. Doing this helps to orient their place in the world – essential if students are going to not only gain a seat at the table but also feel comfortable there. Further, understanding the methods of exclusion in our systems is important; knowing why it is that some voices are valued or remembered over others. However, almost by definition, to do this you need to understand the canon too. You need to know what's included in order to know what is left out. This is why I have argued that we have a duty (to all our students but particularly those from BAME or disadvantaged backgrounds) to offer a curriculum that allows students to access what I have termed the 'broader picture': learning about the canon (or the facts or dominant discourse) but also how this came to be that way. In order to achieve this, there needs to be a conversation in the curriculum between what the traditional canon is made of and what has often been excluded. Considerable thought needs to be given to how this weaves together as a whole narrative, as I believe that it is in this whole that the transformative potential for students and their communities lies. Some curriculum examples can help elucidate this idea.

In history, I do not believe it is enough for our students to simply learn about Britain in the Middle Ages; they must also learn about the cultures and empires across Eurasia, Africa and the Americas at that time: for example, the Moors, the Ottomans, the empires of Mali, Songhai and Benin. Crucially, though, that doesn't mean we stop teaching about the dead white men of the traditional canon. We also need to talk about them, and *Magna Carta*, and the Peasants' Revolt; they brought us these foundational concepts for understanding our parliamentary democracy and to some extent the working class struggle that pervades right up to today. And when we put these ideas together as a whole, this also allows us to engage in some really interesting historical enquiry about the relationship between centre and periphery. Why was it that the Muslim world was so much more developed than Europe in the Middle Ages? And why by the middle of the second millennium had Europe reached an ascendancy? This focus is both academically ambitious – spanning questions of scientific and technological discovery, colonialism and slavery and political systems – as well as potentially politically radical.

This approach is not just relevant for history but for literature and the arts too. When considering the English curriculum, we cannot erase writers of colour, but nor should we deny the foundational place in the world of Dickens, Hardy and Brontë. We need our students to read *Jane Eyre* but we need them to read *Wide Sargasso Sea* too. We have to teach all of it: what has been remembered and what has been forgotten and how this came to be. And yes, some of it is dreary and alienating; but the job of teachers is to bring it alive, make students see the relevance and understand that things beyond their immediate experience can be relevant to them too.

I strongly believe that, as educators, we have a duty to offer all our students, and in particular those from working class or BAME backgrounds, this broader picture. I feel a missionary-like zeal to (paraphrasing Audre Lorde (1984)) use the master's tools to dismantle the master's house. That is, to challenge the status quo by first understanding how it functions and what it excludes. I also believe it is matter of intellectual integrity to insist on reading these voices together, and I believe there is transformative potential for our students in doing this. By understanding how the world works, they also get to have a stake in it. They can see that the world is not something done to them but something they are part of. The goal is that they will also feel that they want to contribute; that this knowledge will enable change. It may make them feel angry about the world, yes, but it must also equip them to take on the challenge of shaping it.

However, what is taught in the classrooms is only part of the issue. To return to Bourdieu, he is clear that the family is the primary unit of socialisation and the role of school is limited. Therefore, if schools in disadvantaged areas are really going to try to match the cultural capital of more advantaged young people, there needs to be a strong extracurricular (or co-curricular) offer.

The academy I mentioned at the start of this chapter had a wonderful programme, paid for in part by the sponsor's own foundation. It was a co-curricular offer that provided an incredible array of opportunities including adventure learning built into the school day. This gave a real chance for students (some of whom had never stepped on uneven ground or spent a night under canvas before) to relate to the natural world and to develop their character and relationship to their self and others in new ways.

However, a 2017 LKMco report – *Learning Away: The State of School Residentials in England 2017* (Menzies et al., 2017) – indicates that this is the exception, not the rule, as pupils in disadvantaged areas have fewer opportunities for residential visits than their more advantaged peers. This disparity eems to me a bigger rallying cry for the left than whether or not some schools have zero tolerance behaviour policies or teach knowledge explicitly. Tentatively, therefore, I suggest that we engage with the healthy debate around curriculum content but save our anger and direct it not at each other, but towards addressing the impact of austerity and the very tangible ways that the funding crisis in our schools is impacting disadvantaged students' opportunities to access their cultural heritage.

Ultimately, the debate about the paternalistic and political nature of education (which is currently played out around curriculum content and discussing which form may or may not be more liberatory in principle) could go on unendingly. Helpful though it is to situate these debates about curriculum in the broader context of critical theory, at some point we (on the left) have to stop and ask ourselves what is pragmatic. Given the short amount of time that schools actually have with their students and given the financial constraints of austerity, I have therefore suggested that to truly contribute to students' cultural capital in a way that is both pragmatic and principled, there needs to be an academic curriculum that offers the broader picture alongside a properly funded co-curricular offer. Instead of arguing amongst ourselves, it might be wise to remember that these debates are productive as long as they don't distract us from doing something real for our students. In my (always partial) position, I have suggested this might be offering them a powerful curriculum that provides a 'broader picture' and fighting for funding for better opportunities outside of the classroom.

References

Benjamin, W. (1969) *Illuminations.* Arendt, H. (ed.) and Zohn, H. (trans.). New York, NY: Schocken Books, pp. 217–252.

Bourdieu, P. (1984) *Distinction: a social critique of the judgement of taste.* Cambridge, MA: Harvard University Press.

Didau, D. (2019) 'Where we're getting curriculum wrong – part 1: cultural capital', *Learning Spy* [Blog]. Retrieved from: www.bit.ly/3eud24e

Lorde, A. (1984) *Sister outsider : essays and speeches.* Trumansburg, NY: Crossing Press.

Lukacs, G. (1971) *The theory of the novel.* Bostock, A. (trans.). London: Merlin Press.

Mansell, W. (2019) 'Ofsted plan to inspect "cultural capital" in schools attacked as elitist', *The Guardian*, 3 September. Retrieved from: https://bit.ly/2VI4RJ5

Menzies, L., Bowen-Viner, K. and Shaw, B. (2017) *Learning away: the state of school residentials in England 2017.* London: LKMco. Retrieved from: www.bit.ly/2wVAiXD

Reid, A. (2018) 'Curriculum, critical theory and conversation: why the right don't need to dominate the discussion', *Parents and Teachers for Excellence* [Blog], 30 October. Retrieved from: www.bit.ly/2Qkhjgf

Young, M. and Lambert, D. (2014) *Knowledge and the future school: curriculum and social justice.* London: Bloomsbury.

Author bio-sketch:

Aurora is an assistant headteacher, safeguarding lead and humanities teacher in Bristol. She studied Anthropology and the Study of Religions at SOAS, London, before joining the Teach First programme and specialising in special educational needs. She is passionate about all things inclusion and believes vehemently in curriculum as a tool for social change.

CREATING A CHALLENGING AND COHERENT CURRICULUM FOR PROGRESS AND PLEASURE

SONIA THOMPSON

St Matthew's C of E Primary School in Nechells is in one of the most deprived areas in Birmingham and the UK. When I became the deputy headteacher (and later on the headteacher), we knew very early on that we could not afford not to have an ambitious curriculum. We knew that if we were ever going to close the attainment gap for children born in an inner city area such as ours, we had to be unflinching in our ambition. In this chapter, I will focus on the why of our curriculum, how our ethos sets the standard for excellence, why and how we celebrate existing capital and build on it and how the teaching of reading and vocabulary underpins our curriculum goals. The chapter concludes with what our next steps will be and why we must ensure that our school remains driven by the need to strive for the best for our children.

Our context, as one of the most deprived areas in the country, demanded that if our children are to have choices, our curriculum needed to be underpinned by a relentless drive for social justice. I see it as our moral imperative to strive to achieve the best if we want our children to be the best. Quite simply, that is our why.

The ethos that underpins our why

Our mottos, vision and values set the standard for our ambitions. Our school ethos means that our curriculum intent is clear. As Mary Myatt recommends, we know what we are offering to our children and the reason why (Myatt, 2018).

Mottos

'With God, nothing is impossible' and 'You are the light of the world'.

Vision

'St Matthew's is a community of learners, planning, pursuing and providing excellence and enjoyment through Christian values. Children are valued for their individuality and heritage. They are supported and motivated to fulfil their potential; in order to meet the challenges of a changing society'.

Values – CAP

C – Courage: Team St Matthew's does not give up. We look back in history to prepare ourselves for the future.

A – Attainment: Team St Matthew's focuses on results and we do whatever it takes to achieve our goals. We push ourselves beyond what we think is possible.

P – Pride: Team St Matthew's values excellence in all that we do. We think and act as our own best selves.

We have enabled our children to live this ethos through the high expectations around behaviour and building their attitudes to learning. Our children want to learn and they love to learn. That's what they tell us. Their eagerness to challenge themselves and learn demanding content is infectious and drives our determination to do whatever we can to realise this.

Over the years, as this ethos has embedded, it has allowed our teachers the uninterrupted space to deliver lessons across all curriculum areas, with explicit content and a strengthening body of robust knowledge.

Building on existing cultural capital and teaching powerful knowledge

At St Matthew's, we all agree that knowledge is power for our children. The context demands that that knowledge be substantive. We have striven and continue to strive to achieve this rigour across all of our curriculum subjects and we know that our outcomes have risen because of this. Our children study classic literature and learn Latin, and learning an instrument and completing a music exam is a right – not a privilege – for our children. We ensure that we seek out the most inspiring people to strengthen and deepen our teachers' subject knowledge and we locate trips and visits to places that our children, within our context, would not ordinarily visit. Our year 6 children have the opportunity to be tour guides in Stratford, supporting real tourists. Visitors are always surprised at how knowledgeable our children are about Shakespeare's birthplace, and even our quietest children blossom. We demand that they have access to the best and we make no apologies for this. We want to open doors for our children and we want them to step through with confidence into a future world where they will hopefully make a huge difference.

In all of this, though, I am mindful of not ever wanting to portray our children as deficit. This is particularly pertinent because the majority of our children are from black and minority ethnic backgrounds, as are many of my teachers. We are strident about the need for there to be a co-existence between (and a deference to) the rich cultural capital that our children and our teachers bring into our school and the rich knowledge and traditions of the country that they are entitled to be exposed to.

The evidence-based work of Luis Moll (Gonzales et al., 2005) has supported us to proudly expose the space within our curriculum to not only acknowledge heritage and culture but to place its deep richness at the heart of our curriculum. Moll refers to 'funds of knowledge' and states that these are the 'rich repositories of accumulated knowledge found present in households and communities'.

We wanted to 'challenge and disrupt taken-for-granted assumptions and perceptions about families' such as ours. We seek to find out about 'personal passions, ways of learning outside school, popular cultural interests and their everyday literacy practices and experiences' (Gonzales et al., 2005). So, at the beginning of each of our subject weeks, children, families and teachers 'share their literacy lives' (Gonzales et al., 2005) and benefit greatly from learning about each other and what make us the humans that we are. Our whole-school theme called 'The Six Ours' enables this to happen. We begin the year with, 'Our Lives, Our Family'; we go onto 'Our Community', Our World', 'Our Passions', 'Our Global Village'; and finally, 'Our Future'.

Moll writes that 'understanding the funds of knowledge within a community and a family is important for a teacher. He/she can tap into this knowledge and use it to help acquire new knowledge' (Gonzales et al., 2005). So at St Matthew's, through the 'Ours', we are able to share stories about our families and culture, including where our families are from and why they came to England. I have shared with the children information about my heritage and the things that I value and that make my culture so rich. Teachers and children have shared pictures of siblings and themselves and our parents have shared stories from their cultures and invited us to share their journeys and learn how this has influenced their current lifestyles. We also have an open-door policy, as well as having a dedicated 'Parents to School Day' as part of our subject weeks. Parents can directly input in to all foundation subject teaching. Cremin et al. (2014a) states that 'many schools view parents primarily as supporters of schoolwork, rather than seeing them as a source of different and/or complementary literacy and learning experiences'. This reciprocity has strengthened our school community and we are all the better for it.

The importance of the national curriculum

The 2014 national curriculum framework for key stages 1 to 4 states that 'the national curriculum provides pupils with an introduction to **the essential knowledge that they need to be educated citizens**. It introduces pupils to **the best that has been thought and said**' (Department for Education, 2014; my emphasis).

Amanda Spielman, when writing about the curriculum in 2018, stated that 'the **vast, accumulated wealth of human knowledge**, and what we choose to pass on to the next generation through teaching in our schools (the curriculum), **must be at the heart of education**' (my emphasis).

At St Matthew's, we agree with both of these quotes, so when we began to re-examine our curriculum, the first thing we did was to read the introductions to each of the subject areas. We quickly unpicked the need for subject distinctiveness. We also identified that we needed a schema that would afford our children the opportunity to experience the connectedness of the curriculum. This meant that senior staff and subject leaders had to establish the coherence within and across subjects. I would describe this as the beginning of our curriculum journey. We went to conferences, spoke to teachers and consultants, read around our subjects, trialled our emerging curriculum in classrooms, got feedback, adjusted and tentatively began to plot it out and roll it out. This also led us to the subject associations, which have over the years (as they have developed stronger materials and support, particularly for primary schools) greatly improved. We also learnt more about cognitive science and memory and how this could underpin our children learning in the way we needed them to learn – and remembering it.

In her blog, Rosalind Walker (also known as Ruth Ashbee, author of chapter 2 in this volume) examines Professor Young's writing (Walker, 2019). She comments on 'the best knowledge being that which is defined by the subject community'. She goes on to say that:

> Powerful knowledge is knowledge that opens things up to students: opportunities, further knowledge, and transcendence of the everyday. Powerful knowledge is typically abstract or rarefied, and will not be picked up by students from their everyday life. It requires expert teaching. It's ambitious, empowering, and beautiful.

Walker eloquently sums up the thoughts underpinning our thinking when constructing our curriculum. For us, it could not be static or fixed; instead, we needed our curriculum to live and breathe powerful knowledge and our context. This meant the diversity of our children and the community that we serve and the need for them to see themselves reflected positively within their curriculum. This was a non-negotiable and has proved to be a powerful driver for us all.

Reading for pleasure and progress as the cornerstone of our curriculum

If 'funds of knowledge' is the head of our school, then reading for pleasure and progress is its heart. We nurture our community of readers, with quality time provided daily. Research has identified pedagogies which develop children's love of reading, so all of our teachers are trained to deliver these well (The Open University, no date). The importance of becoming 'a reader who teaches and a teacher who reads' is one of those pedagogies that has far-reaching consequences. In developing this, we have empowered our teachers to deepen their knowledge of what writers do well. Modelling good independent reading practices also means that our teachers support the development of our children's agency and their independence as readers.

Our school environment crystallises reading for pleasure as a valued and purposeful part of our curriculum. We have also found that the pleasure our children take in reading books of their own choosing extends into the pleasure they find in reading the challenging fiction, non-fiction and poetry of our choice. As Teresa Cremin states, 'The will influences the skill' (Cremin et al., 2014b).

Our direct and explicit approach to the teaching of reading is also underpinned by research. The Education Endowment Fund guidance *Improving Literacy in Key Stage 2* (Higgins et al., 2017) describes the many strands that are woven into skilled reading. It also comments on the research being clear that there is no single approach to teaching reading well. So, at St Matthew's, our teachers use guided, whole-class and independent strategies to teach decoding and language comprehension. We ensure that it is extremely well thought out and well planned, with opportunities for children to retrieve, re-read, practise often and ultimately acquire fluency. Teachers model comprehension strategies and then we move into the application of these strategies (often together), as readers do. It is about deliberate and effortless automaticity and this starts in reception.

This method is based on Doug Lemov's 'close reading' strategies. His book *Reading Reconsidered* (Lemov et al., 2016) challenged my thinking about what children should be reading and empowered us to raise our game. Lemov describes how we should be reading harder texts, reading more non-fiction, writing in response to our reading and close reading (the methodical breaking-down of the language and structure of complex passages) more often. This approach requires an examination of words, sentences, and paragraphs within a text. It also requires knowledge of the text that our teachers will admit they were not used to having or needing. No longer could we pick up texts, skim and scan, read the teacher guide and then teach. Instead it required us to thoroughly understand the themes and authorial intensions within the texts in order to drill down into the deliberate instructional elements of teaching comprehension and vocabulary and the application of these into other areas of the curriculum. This has now become part of our whole-class reading practise.

The other thing that has become normal practice is using non-fiction to both build knowledge and teach knowledge. We use it as a secondary text which we insert to support the children to deepen their understanding of the primary text or the main reader. For example, when reading *War Horse*, we will pair that with a text about posttraumatic stress disorder (PTSD). The idea of shell shock as a direct response to witnessing traumatic events and the fact that it can induce fear, helplessness and horror was incredibly powerful. Through understanding the effects of PTSD, the children were able to discuss and better understand the actions of some of the characters in the book, as well as the horses. For some children, reading the non-fiction piece definitely helped with the absorption (understanding) of the primary text. It also supports their ability to apply this intertextuality to their written responses; quoting meaning from both texts along with their relationships.

The ambition that close reading has inspired in us meant that our year 6 children have confidently responded to highly demanding text-dependent questions around many themes, including heroes and heroism. We have used the works of philosophers such as Friedrich Nietzsche and Thomas Carlyle and discussed the idea of Übermensch (superman). Children have applied their learning to identifying the connectedness of the theme of heroism in other books they have read and programmes they have watched, including *Beowulf*, *Varjak Paw* and *Doctor Who*. They have also discussed the ambiguous nature of these philosophers' arguments and, based on their background knowledge around Christianity, have been able to express preferences for certain philosophers' views over others. This level of discussion would have sat comfortably in a university lecture hall, never mind an inner-city school in Nechells, Birmingham. But my teachers and I just thought, 'Why not?' Our children have as much of a right to this as any other child, and when they are given this diet of challenge, they certainly rise to it and often exceed all expectations.

Now our children approach reading with an added enthusiasm – even those that required additional scaffolds. They recognise its power and use. Children are eager to increase their background knowledge, often reading at home and referencing that reading back in lessons. Our children are reading so much more – both silently and aloud – and we provide even more opportunities for them to be read to. Lemov talks about 'reading road miles' (Lemov et al., 2016), and we have certainly upped ours to the betterment of our readers. The impact of these approaches on the teaching of reading can be measured in both attainment and the surveys, which state that St Matthew's children love reading, for both pleasure and progress.

Why vocabulary matters even more in our curriculum

Although I have previously mentioned vocabulary in this chapter, it was the renewed focus on the ambitiousness of our curriculum that made us confront the harsh reality that the teaching of vocabulary needed greater consistency. We had always taught vocabulary reasonably well in English lessons and had actually done well in reading tests. Yet, within reading and other curriculum sessions, vocabulary teaching was not explicitly and implicitly planned for.

On reflection, I recognised that I needed to develop our teachers' understanding of why we needed to teach vocabulary extremely well. They also needed to understand the pedagogy and use the metalanguage associated with more robust vocabulary instruction. E.D. Hirsch, in an article about comprehension, confirmed this reflection when he explained that overcoming the vocabulary deficit is a huge challenge but that the only way to do it is by 'providing an environment that accelerates the incidentals of vocabulary' (Hirsch, 2003).

Having been on Doug Lemov's reading training, where I was introduced to Isabel Beck et al.'s book *Bringing Words to Life*, I quickly recognised that this was what I had been looking for – something that would afford our children clear and evidence-based vocabulary practices, as well as providing our teachers with 'a fuller understanding of the importance and joyfulness of interest in words' (Beck et al., 2013).

In fact, it has contributed so much more than that. It has made us word-aware, across all subject areas. The impact was such that it has served as a channel for helping us to define what is really meant by learning meanings of new words. Teachers had felt they were doing this, but the book exposed that we most certainly were not – and then helped us to adopt:

- a shared language, when discussing how to robustly and explicitly teach word meaning, from reception to year 6.
- direct teaching activities, which were transferable across the curriculum and must be consistently practised.

Previously, we had addressed vocabulary as it had appeared in the text, and this was often dictated by the words the children did not understand, rather than context-driven vocabulary and words that held the potential to unlock the text. Now, teachers prepare the vocabulary to be taught in advance. They understand the 'tiers' of vocabulary and are clear about which tier needs to be taught when, why and how. Teachers are more confident about developing child-friendly definitions and establishing follow-up activities in order to embed the vocabulary learning. The children are also more eager to use their vocabulary journals and to record and investigate etymology and morphology, which nicely complements our teaching of Latin.

Most importantly of all, our teachers understand that their efforts, in delivering robust vocabulary instruction, can advance children's access to the curriculum. In our reception class, this has resulted in timetabled explicit vocabulary sessions, using linked stories and non-fiction texts; and in year 6 RE, tier-3 words such as 'transfiguration' can be used and applied in discussions and in written explanations. It has also served as an early win for us when supporting our children, who often come in to school 18 months behind in language development.

In his book *Closing the Vocabulary Gap*, Alex Quigley states, 'It is our privilege to offer the children we teach a wealth of words. We should seize the opportunity' (Quigley, 2018). He also comments that 'vocabulary should be a priority for teachers and their continuous professional development'. At St Matthew's, we have certainly seen the benefit of this CPD. In empowering our teachers, the opportunities for our children to understand word meanings and then go on to apply them have had noticeable results. This has further cemented the ambitiousness of our curriculum.

What matters to us as our curriculum journey continues?
We will continue to:

- put reading for pleasure and progress at the heart of our school.
- create opportunities to build on our children's existing cultural capital (funds of knowledge).
- teach powerful subject-distinctive knowledge for long-term learning – building/deepening background knowledge – using all subject areas.
- embed drama and oracy across the curriculum.
- develop context-driven vocabulary and language learning.
- provide the best subject-specific CPD for our middle leaders and teachers.
- reduce excessive teacher workload through the use of reduced marking and using recommended, respected and tested schemes of work.

Conclusion
In drawing this chapter to an end, I hope that our vision for our curriculum and what we see as the purpose of education at St Matthew's Primary School is clear. Our ambitiousness for our children and for ourselves as educators has brought us so far – but we cannot and will not be complacent. We still have some way to go. As previously stated, our curriculum cannot be fixed. It must be responsive to our context and our community and, most importantly, it must espouse social justice. Our curriculum must continue to build on the richness that is already there and take it deeper and wider, so that our children, from Nechells, Birmingham, can soar to heights that not even we (with all our ambitiousness) think is possible.

References
Beck, I. L., McKeown, M. G. and Kucan, L. (2013) *Bringing words to life: robust vocabulary instruction.* New York, NY: The Guildford Press.

Cremin, T., Mottram, M., Collins, F. M., Powell, S. and Drury, R. (2014a) *Researching literacy lives: building communities between home and school.* Abingdon: Routledge.

Cremin, T., Mottram, M., Collins, F. M., Powell, S. and Safford, K. (2014b) *Building communities of engaged readers: reading for pleasure.* Abingdon: Routledge.

Department for Education (2014) *National curriculum in England: framework for key stages 1 to 4.* London: The Stationery Office. Retrieved from: www.bit.ly/2Wrt60h

Gonzales, N., Moll, L. C. and Amanti, C. (2005) *Funds of knowledge: theorizing practices in households, communities, and classrooms.* Mahwah, NJ: Lawrence Erlbaum Associates.

Higgins, S., Martell, T., Waugh, D., Henderson, P. and Sharples, J. (2017) *Improving literacy in key stage 2.* London: Education Endowment Foundation. Retrieved from: www.bit.ly/2w4ixpa

Hirsch, E. D. (2003) 'Reading comprehension requires knowledge', *American Educator* 27 (1) pp. 10–13, 16–22, 28–29, 48.

Lemov, D., Driggs, C. and Woolway, E. (2016) *Reading reconsidered: a practical guide to rigorous literacy instruction*. San Francisco, CA: Jossey-Bass.

Myatt, M. (2018) *The curriculum: gallimaufry to coherence*. Woodbridge: John Catt Educational.

The Open University (no date) 'Reading for pleasure pedagogy', *Research Rich Pedagogies* [Website]. Retrieved from: www.bit.ly/2x1gJgz

Quigley, A. (2018) *Closing the vocabulary gap*. Abingdon: Routledge.

Spielman, A. (2018) *Curriculum and the new education inspection framework*. Department for Education. London: The Stationery Office. Retrieved from: www.bit.ly/2W1IVJ5

Walker (2019) 'Powerful knowledge: what it is, why it's important, and how to make it happen in your school', *The Fruits Are Sweet* [Blog], 18 October. Retrieved from www.bit.ly/2UeCjpW

Author bio-sketch:

Sonia Thompson is the headteacher at St Matthew's C of E Primary Teaching and Research School in Nechells, Birmingham, which was the first winner of the Egmont Reading for Pleasure School of the Year award in 2018. Sonia is passionate about evidence-based practice, including curriculum, reading and reading for pleasure. She has spoken about these topics at various conferences, including at Peters and researchED. She is an advisor for the OU/UKLA Research Rich Pedagogies website. Sonia is a member of the UKLA National Council and is an EmpathyLab judge. She tweets as @son1bun.

CURRICULUM COHERENCE: HOW BEST TO DO IT?

NEIL ALMOND

In his pamphlet *Principled Curriculum Design*, Dylan Wiliam makes the point that 'the word "curriculum" has no generally agreed meaning' (Wiliam, 2013, p. 7). At its most basic level, it is the content, the 'what', that should be taught to students. I am going to argue that principled curriculum design needs to include the careful sequencing of that content so that it creates a coherent journey for our students to travel on that begins with them being novices within the subject domains and guides them on the path to becoming more expert. At the start, students' understanding is shallow; but gradually and progressively, over time, more and more connections are made both explicitly within the structure of what is taught and internally as students' own schemata become more sophisticated as a result of this deliberate sequencing. This deliberate journey to connectedness forms what is often referred to as the 'intended curriculum' and it is this element of curriculum that this chapter will explore.

The revised national curriculum for England, introduced by the coalition government in 2014, was deliberately slimmed down to allow teachers the professional judgement to design a curriculum with the needs of their pupils in mind (Gove, 2013). However, many teachers were not trained in curricular design and so many fall into two traps when planning lessons.

Grant Wiggins and Jay McTighe recognise two errors often made by teachers in curriculum design which they call the 'twin sins' (Wiggins and McTighe, 2005). The first of these is activity-based design. Here, students are engaged with often hands-on learning that lacks any academic rigour and fails to take account of a wider learning journey. Put simply, teachers plan activities to engage learners where the activity becomes the learning. For example, after being told a story about the Roman victory over the Iceni queen Boudica at the Battle of Watling Street, students could be given the simple activity to dress as Roman and Celtic warriors, act out the battle and write a newspaper report on it. The danger with such activities is that students spend far too much cognitive energy on selecting the correct colour tunic and do not pay a great deal of attention to the actual learning of the historical content of the story. (Not to mention embedding the misconception that newspapers and mass literacy were common at the time.) It is this approach to design where we must ask questions such as: 'What is the purpose of this activity?'; 'What knowledge are they demonstrating?'; 'Does this activity match the learning outcomes that were planned?'; 'Is this an effective use of time?'

The second 'sin' Wiggins and McTighe identify is 'coverage'. Here the teacher rushes through set content in a heroic effort to cover all the necessary requirements within a set time due to external pressures such as days lost to whole-school events and celebrations of national events. Because of this, learning is rushed or incomplete and will likely to lead to what the cognitive scientist Daniel Willingham calls shallow knowledge. This is when 'students have some understanding of the material but their understanding is limited' (Willingham, 2009, p 72). Because of this limited understanding, it is highly probable that students will be unable to transfer the knowledge learnt in these lessons; therefore, they are unlikely to develop a greater understanding of the content – especially if it is revisited later on. For example, to draw on the Roman example from the first 'sin', if we ensured that students were able to learn the importance of the location of the Battle of Watling Street, we could deepen that knowledge when later learning about the Vikings and Anglo-Saxons: Watling Street is mentioned in the Treaty of Alfred and Guthrum as the boundary of the Danelaw, marking which land belonged to the Vikings and which to Anglo-Saxon kingdoms. In addition, as Watling Street began at Dover, its importance in early trade could also be examined. Edgware Road, in north-west London, is approximately contiguous with the original route of Watling Street, which is why this particular road is straight for around ten miles (Higgs, 2017). It now marks the boundary for the Camden, Brent, Barnet and Harrow boroughs in London. If we focus on 'coverage' as a main driver for our curriculum, then this nuance and ability to deepen our knowledge risks being lost. I would like to stipulate here that these errors are by no means the fault of any individual or school but simply a reflection of what can occur in classrooms today.

The case for cohesion

Before one embarks on curriculum design, there needs to be pause for thought as to what you want the curriculum to achieve, particularly what the end goal is. What do we hope our students will learn and remember? In contrast to the idea of shallow knowledge mentioned by Willingham, there is also deep knowledge. A student with deep knowledge not only knows more but can see the links between what they know and how new learning connects to prior learning. In other words, they do not just understand part of something; they understand the whole (Willingham, 2009). The benefit of deeper knowledge is that this knowledge can be transferred into a greater number of situations – essentially deepening the meaning of concepts and ideas that we already understand through new examples and occurrences. In order to achieve this deeper understanding, it must connect together previous shallow knowledge. Deeper connections and understanding of concepts and ideas only become meaningful once the learner has integrated them into an already present but shallower understanding of those concepts (Furst, 2019). Therefore, the role of curriculum is to take learners' shallow knowledge and understanding of a topic and make it deeper. For this to happen, the curriculum needs to be planned carefully so that key ideas and concepts are continuously revisited, remembered and built upon. If our content is not sufficiently sequenced and built on what has been truly learnt, resulting in a change in long-term memory, any new content will not be remembered and therefore cannot be used to think critically in different contexts. For example, students not secure in understanding the location of the equator and the climate associated with it will struggle to explain why it is that tropical rainforests are humid and appear predominantly along the equator. Students who already understand those associated details about the equator would be far more likely to make the link with tropical rainforests. As Dylan Wiliam writes, the 'purpose of curriculum is to build up the content of long-term memory so that when students are asked to think, they are able to think in more powerful ways' (Wiliam, 2018).

An analogy to remember: curriculum as box set

Analogies are a powerful tool for learning. The reason for this is that they connect ideas that we do not know or fully understand to prior knowledge we do know well and help us make sense of the new material we wish to know (Willingham, 2009). The analogy this chapter deploys is one that everyone should be familiar with – that of a television box set.

Consider for a moment the television show *The Simpsons*. While the viewer needs to give some attention to getting to know the characters and the relationships between them, there is certainly no overarching plot for the series and no sub-plot within a season to attend to; however many episodes we watch, our knowledge and understanding does not get very much deeper. Rather, we just accumulate more shallow knowledge as we watch each episode.

As a result of this lack of depth, what is truly wonderful about the series is that you do not have to have seen the episodes in chronological order or in a particular sequence. The watcher is free to pick any episode off the shelf and can no doubt enjoy the episode but will not be required to think too deeply about it. As each episode does not build on what has come before it, having a depth of prior knowledge is not necessary. Figure 1 demonstrates what this looks like when the box set analogy is used to show lessons planned as a series of only loosely connected one-offs in similar fashion to *The Simpsons*.

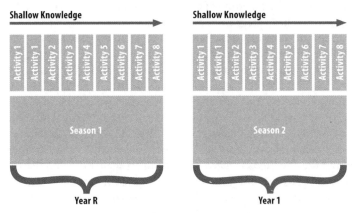

Figure 1: A curriculum designed out of shallow understanding where previous ideas and concepts are not revisited.

Now consider the television series *Game of Thrones* or *Line of Duty*. In contrast to *The Simpsons*, there is an overarching plot to the whole series; there is purpose and there is a clear thread that binds the seasons together. Not only this, but within the individual seasons, there are sub-plots which tie the episodes of that season together. Within each episode (or two, if the deliberate stylistic choice of a cliffhanger has been made), there is a plot that is resolved which means the episode has its own merit; a short-term purpose of being there. Each episode deepens our understanding until the plot of the season is resolved. This is why one cannot simply watch and understand any single episode from such a series as we lack the necessary prior learning from previous episodes to make any meaning from the random episode. The plots within each episode are a vital part of understanding the plot of the season, which in turn is crucial to solving the overarching plot of the series. Although a quick, initial summary – what is known in the TV trade as 'the previously' – may put us on the correct path and give us a bare minimum of understanding, viewers that have attended and thought deeply about each episode, the actions of the characters and events, will get a much deeper understanding of character motivation and plot choice. It is a delicate, intricate and purposeful web of knowledge that gradually deepens and all links up together to create a cohesive journey.

But what does this have to do with the intended curriculum?

Now imagine the 'episodes' as lessons; the whole series as a subject from the national curriculum and each season being a year of schooling. Working with these ideas, we can think of curriculum as a well-written television series, like *Game of Thrones* or *Line of Duty*. There is a grand and complicated story arch that covers the whole series – in a school context this would be the curriculum a child experiences from reception to year 6, or from year 7 to year 11, or even into year 13. In an ideal world, probably only possible in all-through schools or multi-academy trusts that span both phases, the curriculum builds cumulatively from the very start of reception to the very end of year 13. This curriculum is then broken down by year group – corresponding to a season using our box set analogy. Within each individual season lies its own narrative plot, which is worthy in its own right and is resolved by the end of the season – but can also set the scene for what is to come or play a part in the resolution of the overarching story arch. In an educational context, each season provides the core knowledge and understanding required in each year group in order to successfully progress and understand the subsequent seasons that will follow. In other words, it takes new ideas and learning and gradually increases the complexity of those ideas so that a child's knowledge goes from shallower to deeper over the course of their schooling. The higher up the school you teach, the more important it is to know the intricate details of what has been taught previously; when it comes to delivering your lessons, you can bring previous ideas that may have seemed irrelevant at the time back to the forefront. The lower down the school, the more you need to be aware of the final outcome of the whole series so you can weave the initial ideas and introduce the correct (but initially shallow) knowledge into your lessons which can then be picked up and subsequently built on by the teachers further up the school.

Coherent curriculum design is a whole-school enterprise. This is what is meant when you hear the phrase 'curriculum is the progression model' – students are remembering what they need to know from previous years and using it in order to make sense of what they learn in the coming years as their understanding deepens. With time, certain aspects are brought to mind effortlessly. The student may not even be aware that they are remembering them as such, as the knowledge has now become an automatic part of their thinking apparatus. This is the same as how, when watching a complicated box set early on, you might need to consciously call to mind who each character is and how they relate to others, or ask annoying questions of your viewing companions. By season two, such knowledge is deeply ingrained and recalled automatically.

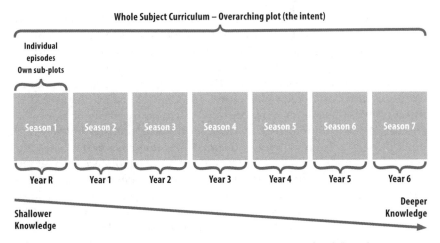

Figure 2: A model of curriculum that demonstrates how knowledge within a subject can go from shallow to deep in a coherent curriculum.

How best to create this cohesion?

Both the activity- and coverage-driven curriculum as described by Wiggins and McTighe (2005) are the result of making decisions about curriculum design starting at the beginning of the learning journey. When planning begins at the beginning, it is difficult to have a shared understanding – or indeed any understanding at all – of the shared final outcomes or how best to get there. The writers of complex box set series do not start writing episode one and then continue writing from the basis of that episode and see where it takes them, least of all because it may not be the same person writing each episode. There is rich discussion about the storyline and sub-plots, with key events and details meticulously planned so all writers know what is happening, when it is happening and why it is happening. A builder does not begin the foundations before consulting the blueprints for how the house will look when it's finished. Teachers must do the same when building and writing their curriculum – start at the end. To some teachers, this is a rather paradoxical idea; but it becomes obvious once you consider the previous analogies. However, simply getting teachers to select an area of study from the national curriculum and asking them to think backwards will still not deliver the coherence we are after.

It is good to think of curriculum design at a macro level and micro level. The macro level refers to the distribution of the attainment targets for the subjects from the national curriculum and sequencing these into a coherent order. For example, it makes little sense to teach the history of the Great Fire of London at key stage 1 before children have a wider sense of where London is and its status within the United Kingdom in geography. Ensuring that the curriculum is sequenced in such a way is the first step to securing coherence across the curriculum. Victoria Morris, a teacher at St Matthias School in Tower Hamlets, East London has produced useful documents that can help schools plan the curriculum at this macro level for history and geography. These are available at www.bit.ly/2U2CoOF. For the other subjects, primary school subject leaders might need to research and tap into the expertise of secondary colleagues to help them sequence the attainment targets of the other national curriculum subjects. All teachers, regardless of phase taught, would also benefit from using their respective subject associations.

Once this is done, consider the concepts that will be revisited over again. These subject-based concepts must take students out of their normal lived experience and demonstrate to them the interrelatedness of ideas which can lead to intellectual development; it is these concepts that drive curriculum, though they must be connected to content (Young and Lambert, 2014). In the box set analogy, these concepts are the themes that are represented throughout the series.

For example, when mapping the concepts of 'democracy', it may look something like figure 3. Democracy may first be encountered in reception through the idea of rules that must be followed in the classroom. This could then be visited again in year 1 when studying the Great Fire of London and learning that it was the king who made all the rules. In year 2, children could look at the work of the suffragette Emily Davison and the sacrifices the movement made for women to have the vote. Before learning about the impact of the Romans in Britain, it would be worth giving some background information on Rome, detailing how it went from a republic, with a form of democratic representation, to an empire. This could be built on furthermore in year 4 when learning about the wonders of the Ancient Greeks, where democracy could be compared and contrasted between the city states of Athens and Sparta. To promote chronological understanding, in year 5 the Anglo-Saxons and the Vikings could be studied, and we could bring to attention the fact that the territories under Anglo-Saxon control were ruled by kings. Viking culture, on the other hand, allowed for free men to participate in meetings called 'things' and to vote on important decisions. Finally, in year 6, students could look at the work of Martin Luther King and the civil rights movement's struggle for equality and the right to vote. These units should not be seen in isolation. Because it has been carefully planned, each time democracy appears on the curriculum, teachers can ask students what they remember about this concept from previous years (and offer meaningful prompts if they have forgotten) before deepening their understanding of the concept.

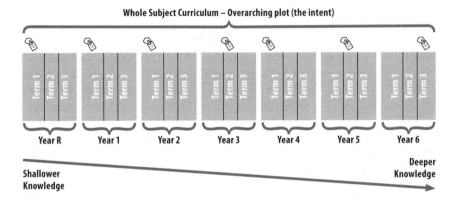

Figure 3: A model of how the concept of democracy may be mapped in a history curriculum at a macro level.

After this stage, you can begin to look at the curriculum on the micro level. This is detailing what happens within a series of lessons but in greater detail so that learning episodes – or lessons – can be created.

There are three crucial steps to consider when planning a succinct and coherent curriculum at the micro level:

1. Be extremely clear as to what the end-of-unit result will be – what will the students know?
2. Express clearly how that final outcome will be produced – how will the students apply their learning in a meaningful way that respects the subject discipline?
3. Break down what that final outcome looks like into manageable chunks to teach during lessons – how will you get the students there?

It looks simple when laid out this way – but rest assured that it can be incredibly complex. For primary school teachers in particular, it is worth remembering that this would have to be replicated for all national curriculum subjects – no easy feat giving that we are generalists in a time when understanding the subject and its associated knowledge is being called for. It is worth looking at these three points in more detail.

Be extremely clear as to what the end-of-unit result will be

The overarching plot for a whole subject should be to learn the curriculum. What teachers should consider is what the sub-plots look like across a term when a subject is being taught. By identifying what the end result will be, the teacher will have clarity and an end goal to work towards. For example, the end goal in a unit of history on the Romans could be understanding the changes the Romans brought to Britain and the response of some native Britons to that change through source analysis. Seen at a macro level, understanding is still shallow; viewed from a micro level, children have moved from a very shallow acquisition of initially disjointed pieces of knowledge to a much more joined-up, deeper understanding. Clarity is provided as teachers know what to include in their lesson and, perhaps more importantly, what not to include. While learning about the gladiatorial games that took place in the Colosseum would be interesting and engaging, it would serve no purpose within this unit. To a busy teacher, this is helpful as it significantly reduces the amount of content we need to learn and gives us a clear basis on which to improve our subject knowledge within the unit.

Express clearly how that final outcome will be produced

With the final outcomes decided, now we can decide how the final outcome will be produced. To extend the example above, students may write an argument explaining what changes took place in Roman Britain and whether they believe the evidence leads us to conclude these changes resulted in positive or negative outcomes. It would be helpful and add further clarity if teachers themselves produced their own examples of these final outcomes to share with the students. This will help solidify the teacher's thinking of what to teach as well provide a high-quality model for students to aspire to. Of course, teachers will also need to plan opportunities for retrieval practice to ensure that the content leading up to this final outcome is sufficiently learnt and understood and so available for thinking with.

Break down what that final outcome looks like into manageable chunks to teach during lessons

Here we can incorporate Rosenshine's second principle of instruction – to present novel information in small steps with student practice at each step (Rosenshine, 2012). These small steps should form the basis for our lessons. Again, plotting these lessons starting at the end is key here, not only for time management, but to ensure that the lessons build on each other and are coherent. This will lead to greater meaning-making and support knowledge acquisition and the journey from shallower to deeper learning. Ensuring that there are key objectives for each lesson and that the work set during the lessons matches the objectives is important if we want the core content to be remembered. Furthermore, we can tap into the box set analogy again and apply it to this stage on the curriculum process. Many series like those mentioned above will start each episode with a short recap of what has happened in previous episodes: 'the previously'. The content shown during this part of the show is not accidental; very deliberate detail has been selected to prompt and bring important information from previous episodes and seasons back into working memory. We can and should make the same choices in our teaching and carefully select detail to recap at the start of our lessons that can help embed and promote long-term retention of new knowledge. At this point, we can bring back previous concepts studied across the subject to deepen links between new and old learning.

References

Ericsson, A. and Pool, R. (2016) *Peak: how to master almost anything.* Toronto: Penguin Random House.

Furst, E. (2019) 'Meaning first', *Teaching with learning in mind* [Blog]. Retrieved from www.bit.ly/3d98Hmu

Gove, M. (2013) *Education reform: new national curriculum for schools* [Statement to parliament]. Department for Education. London: The Stationery Office. Retrieved from: www.bit.ly/3dcgRu6

Higgs, J. (2017) *Watling Street: travels through Britain and its ever-present past.* London: Hachette.

Rosenshine, B. (2012) 'Principles of instruction: research-based strategies that all teachers should know', *American Educator* 36 (1) pp. 12–19, 39.

Schmidt, W. and Prawat, R. (2006) 'Curriculum coherence and national control of education: issue or non-issue?', *Journal of Curriculum Studies* 38 (6) pp. 641–658.

Wiggins, G. P. and McTighe, J. (2005) *Understanding by design.* 2nd edn. Alexandria, VA: Association of Supervision and Curriculum Development.

Wiliam, D. (2013) *Principled curriculum design.* London: SSAT (The Schools Network) Limited.

Wiliam, D. (2018) *Creating the schools our children need: why what we're doing now won't help much (and what we can do instead).* West Palm Beach, FL: Learning Sciences International.

Willingham, D. T. (2009) *Why don't students like school? A cognitive scientist answers questions about how the mind works and what it means for the classroom.* Hoboken, NJ: John Wiley & Sons.

Young, M. and Lambert, D. (2014) *Knowledge and the future school: curriculum and social justice.* London: Bloomsbury.

Author bio-sketch:

Neil Almond is currently in his sixth year in the profession working as a lead teacher at the Woodland Academy Trust, where he helps schools develop teaching and learning and build strong curricula for the students the schools serve. He is passionate about applying educational research in the classroom and has spoken on this topic at researchED events. He would like to dedicate this chapter to his late grandfather Roland George Almond, who always told him to be his own man and follow his passions.

His Twitter handle is @Mr_AlmondED and he blogs at nutsaboutteaching. wordpress.com

CURRICULUM BUILDING IN A PRIMARY SCHOOL
A CASE STUDY

ANDREW PERCIVAL

For years, I believed that the role of curriculum leader in a primary school was similar to a croupier in a casino. You took the content from the national curriculum, shuffled the deck and then dealt the cards out to teachers so that everyone had an equal hand. The year 4 teacher was perhaps dealt mountains in geography, Ancient Egypt in history and painting in art, while the year 6 teacher was pleased with their hand comprising World War II, evolution and volcanoes. As a curriculum leader, I tried to deal cards that might make a 'happy family' – those studying Ancient Greece in history might also study the geography of the country and read some of the famous myths through the English curriculum. Teachers then took these broad topic headings and it was up to them to decide the finer detail of the curriculum that would eventually be taught.

(This all seemed perfectly sensible until we began asking pupils what they remembered from their studies in each subject area. When our history leader asked pupils what they had recently learned from their study of World War II, they easily recalled making Anderson shelters out of corrugated cardboard and tasting the weekly food rations but couldn't remember how, for example, the Treaty of Versailles contributed to the onset of war. We had certainly provided some sustenance for their episodic memories – their memory of context-dependent autobiographical events – but left their context-free semantic memory on fairly reduced rations.)

With their clutch of topics in hand, teachers were left to plan a sequence of lessons based on their own personal preferences and their conception of the core content to be taught. As the lessons were generally activity-based, they could frequently stand alone as discrete sessions without having to consider their sequencing too deeply. Often these lessons were interchangeable with each other. When teaching the unit on World War II, if a teacher didn't have the resources ready for the lesson on food rationing then they could simply teach the evacuees session and the rationing activity could be slotted in later. We considered the teaching sequence as if it were a compilation of interesting gobbets about World War II rather than a sequence of content building a coherent understanding of the topic. Our thinking was constrained by the belief that the unit of delivery – the lesson – should also be the primary unit of planning. As David Didau states, 'Dividing schemes of work into individual lessons distracts teachers from concentrating on what is to be learned over time' (Didau, 2015). We eventually realised that we needed to think more carefully about the sequence of learning over a longer period of time rather than simply at the level of the individual lesson.

While we had broad curriculum plans in place, there was little detail to support the careful acquisition of the complex web of interconnected knowledge that we desired. This web or schema, as it is often referred to as in psychology, maps out the organisation of current knowledge about people, places, objects and events and the relationships between them. While individuals construct their own unique schema from their personal experiences of the world, we identified that we needed to support schema development through a more carefully planned sequence of knowledge. This would give pupils every opportunity to extend and connect what they knew in meaningful ways. We were well aware that, without a rich store of knowledge to draw upon, pupils would find it difficult, if not impossible, to develop important attributes such as creativity and the ability to think critically about the content of the curriculum. As Dylan Wiliam claims, 'The big mistake we have made … is to assume that if we want students to be able to think, then our curriculum should give our students lots of practice in thinking. This is a mistake because what our students need is more to think *with*' (Wiliam, 2018).

A key consideration of schema development is the prior knowledge that pupils bring to their learning. The aphorism derived from the Gospel of Matthew (and often known as the Matthew effect) – 'the rich get richer and the poor get poorer' – is certainly true of learning. As Shing and Brod state, 'Prior knowledge facilitates memory for incoming information because it provides a structure into which the new information can be integrated' (Shing and Brod, 2016). This leads us to the idea that knowledge is 'sticky' and that the more you know, the more easily you can know more. Could a curriculum be deliberately structured in order to ensure that prior knowledge is acquired and subsequently activated to secure new information? How might we construct a curriculum so that concepts in geography such as 'sustainability' and 'region' are understood, not as memorised dictionary definitions, but as a well-connected schema with multiple contexts to add nuance to meaning and concrete examples to strengthen the concept. The more nuanced the concept, the more likely it can be used to think critically. Our ability to think critically about sustainability, for example, will be greatly enhanced if we know about how sustainability has been attempted in several different contexts.

We started to hear about schools who were using the findings from cognitive science to make strategic decisions about the structure and content of their curriculum. Schools were doing this in a way that built a strong 'house of cards' from a firm foundation with carefully planned threads running through to develop pupils' schema in an explicit way.

As we began to develop our curriculum approach, our ideas coalesced around five broad principles:

1. Acquisition of knowledge and cultural literacy is at the heart of the curriculum.
2. Knowledge is specified in meticulous detail.
3. Knowledge is acquired in long-term memory.
4. Knowledge is carefully sequenced over time.
5. Knowledge is organised into clearly defined subject disciplines.

Acquisition of knowledge and cultural literacy is at the heart of the curriculum

In the book *Why Knowledge Matters*, American professor of education E.D. Hirsch sets out his arguments for a curriculum centred around the acquisition of knowledge (Hirsch, 2016). He draws attention to the striking evidence from the French education system comparing outcomes under a knowledge-based curriculum in the early 1980s to that of the skills-based curriculum of the 1990s onwards. Using data drawn from literacy and maths tests taken by the population of ten-year-olds in France, he demonstrates that under both systems, children from lower socioeconomic groups perform worse than their peers, on average. The striking feature of the dataset is that, under the skills-based approach, the more disadvantaged children fall further behind than their more advantaged peers. However, this gap is significantly reduced under the knowledge-based curriculum, where all pupils achieve at a higher standard. Hirsch argues that this is because children from more wealthy backgrounds perhaps acquire knowledge in the home more readily and the children from lower socioeconomic groups rely more on schools to provide this knowledge of the world. Hirsch claims the change in policy 'deprived poor children of the enabling knowledge that rich children had acquired from their home environments' (2016).

As well as orienting our curriculum towards essential knowledge, we considered how we could further develop pupils' cultural literacy through our curricular choices. How could we support pupils to access a broad cultural education to enable them to understand, participate in and ultimately contribute to the world they live in? So, while our art curriculum primarily focuses on developing pupils' ability to draw and paint, we wanted to ensure they had awareness of significant works of art steeped in cultural significance. We established a list of 30 paintings that we wanted our pupils to be able to identify and understand the historical provenance and artistic significance of.

In English, we reviewed the texts studied in the curriculum and removed some of the more recent texts selected solely because of their relevance to the humanities curriculum. In their place, we introduced a wider range of classic texts including some pre-20th-century literature. Texts such as 'The Selfish Giant', *Alice's Adventures in Wonderland* and *The Hobbit* provided rich opportunities not only to explore the use of language but to enrich the cultural experience of our pupils with stories that have stood the test of time.

How might this approach manifest itself in less overtly knowledge-based subjects such as physical education? Reflecting on the content of the PE curriculum, we removed some of the generic skills-based 'multi-sports' content and introduced more focused study of specific sports. For example, when studying cricket, our pupils learn a simple version of the rules of the game, understand a little of its heritage and the achievements of some of the significant players. Alongside this, we also teach children vocabulary and phrases related to the sport. They learn about the multiple meanings of the term 'wicket' and what an umpire does as well as understanding that having 'a good innings' has a wider meaning beyond the confines of the sport itself. Of course, they spend a lot of time developing their catching, throwing and batting ability too!

We made some larger decisions about the content of the curriculum such as substituting our modern foreign language, Spanish, with an ancient language, Latin, to capitalise on etymology, grammar and cultural literacy opportunities that are an inherent part of the study of classical antiquity.

We were acutely aware that there were many elements of cultural literacy that we had overlooked in our curriculum and so we developed a cycle of assemblies that would ensure a wider cultural appreciation. These included notable stories which we felt all 11-year-olds should know and be able to recall before they leave primary school. These included the stories of significant events such as the sinking of the *Titanic* and the extinction of the dodo; myths and legends from the UK such as King Arthur and Robin Hood; and the achievements of great inventors such as the Wright brothers and Leonardo da Vinci.

Knowledge is specified in meticulous detail

When deciding how we should set out the content of the curriculum, we took heed of the findings from Barak Rosenshine's widely read paper 'Principles of Instruction'. In it, he states that 'the procedure of first teaching in small steps and then guiding student practice represents an appropriate way of dealing with the limitations of our working memory' (Rosenshine, 2012). The idea of building a curriculum consisting of small steps to be mastered made sense. What if we could construct a curriculum with each concept broken down into granular items of knowledge to be mastered to ensure a deeper understanding of the content being studied? Providing the teacher with a clear overview of the precise knowledge pupils will learn then frees them from having to determine content themselves. This, in turn, enables them to focus on deciding the most effective ways to explain the content to pupils; how to adapt their teaching in response to feedback and how to identify and support those who need further challenge.

Taking broad statements from the national curriculum, we began to identify the core knowledge needed to develop a robust schema. For example, the fairly straightforward statement in the year 4 science curriculum 'recognise that vibrations from sounds travel through a medium to the ear' can be broken down into multiple smaller steps to be mastered, giving specific examples to support learning (see next page).

Know that sounds are **generated** when an object **vibrates**.
Know that to vibrate means to shake with repeated small quick movements.
Know that some of the **energy** from the vibrating object is **transferred** to the air, making the air **particles** vibrate.
Know that the vibration travels through the air to our ear in a **wave**.
Know that sound travels in a wave where vibrating particles push against the particles next to them and cause them to vibrate **in succession**.
Know that metal vibrates when it is struck (e.g. tuning fork).
Know what it feels like to touch a vibrating **tuning fork**.
Know that striking a tuning fork causes the air around the fork to vibrate.
Know that **vocal cords** inside our throat vibrate when we speak.
Know what vibrations in our throat feel like when speaking or humming.
Know that sound waves can travel through **solids** (such as metal, stone and wood), **liquids** (such as water) and **gases** (such as the mixture of gases we call **air**).
Know that sound cannot travel in outer space as there is no gas for it to travel through.
Know that sound waves are **detected** in the ear by humans and that the brain **interprets** this as the sounds we hear.
Know that sound travels more slowly than light travels.
Know that this explains why we hear **thunder** after seeing a **flash of lightning**.
Case study: whale song
Know that **whales** can **communicate** over many **miles** underwater.
Know that they communicate through a combination of clicks, whistles and pulsing sounds.
Know that this is usually called '**whale song**'.
Know that some whale song can be heard over 100 miles away from the **source**.
Know that **ambient noise** created by humans (such as boats and machines in the water) can cause difficulties for whales trying to communicate.
Know what whale song sounds like.

Excerpt from year 4 science curriculum unit on sound. Key vocabulary is written in bold to indicate that these words/concepts should be understood by the pupils in the context given.

In order to set each unit of work in its wider context within the curriculum, we prefaced each unit with a description of the context for study. This helps teachers to quickly see what has gone before and what is coming next in order to enrich their teaching and provide valuable reference points to support pupils' conceptual development.

On the opposite page is the full year 1 history unit of work on the Great Fire of London.

The Great Fire of London year 1 (spring term 1)
Context for study
This unit is one of the first history units that pupils study and, as such, there is limited prior knowledge to activate. This unit comes after a study of the history of transport in reception. Pupils should know that most travel was by foot at this time – it was around 150 years before Stephenson's *Rocket* (1829), which they should be familiar with. The Great Fire of London comes after the time of Pieter Bruegel the Elder (c. 1525–1530 to 1569), which pupils studied previously in year 1. They will have some understanding of what life was like during the 16th century from Bruegel's paintings, and this can be built upon as they move into the 17th century to study the Great Fire. The knowledge acquired in this unit will help year 2 pupils in history when studying the Gunpowder Plot and in the geography unit on London, specifically with reference to London landmarks such as St Paul's Cathedral and the River Thames.

Knowledge content
Know that the **Great Fire of London** occurred in **1666**.
Know the location of **London** on a map of the UK.
Know that buildings were mostly made from **wood, straw and pitch**.
Know that pitch is a tar-like substance that protects the wood from water damage.
Know that pitch is **flammable**.
Know that the buildings were very close together to save space.
Know that the previous **summer** had been very hot and there had been very little rain. This meant that the buildings would catch fire easily.
Know that there was no real trained **firefighting** service in London at the time.
Know that people used fire to cook and for light.
Know that Thomas Farriner's **bakery** in Pudding Lane was probably the **source** of the fire as the oven was still burning overnight.
Know that the Great Fire of London started on Sunday 2nd September 1666.
Know that there was a strong wind which helped the fire to spread.
Know that **Samuel Pepys** was a man living in London at the time.
Know that he wrote a **diary** describing the fire.
Know that this is one of the most important **sources** of information about the fire.
Know that we often learn about the past from things people wrote at the time, including diaries.
Know what Samuel Pepys looked like.
Know that people tried to stop the fire by pulling down houses (called a **firebreak**).
Know that people tried to put out the fire with simple firefighting equipment including buckets of water, but the fire was too strong.
Know that the **River Thames** stopped the fire spreading to the **south**.
Know that by Thursday 6th September 1666 all the fires had been put out.
Know that the fire destroyed many homes and famous buildings including **St Paul's Cathedral**.
Know that a **cathedral** is a large and important church.
Know what St Paul's Cathedral looks like in modern times.
Know that the **monarch** at the time was called **King Charles II**.
Know that, after the fire, he wanted to **rebuild** London and improve it with wide streets, beautiful parks and no overcrowding.
Know that in 1668 new rules were put in place that said that buildings had to be made of **stone** and **brick** to stop a similar fire happening again.
Know that streets were built wider so that fires could not spread so easily.
Know that, after the fire, London **Fire Brigade** was set up to stop this happening again.
Know that a **monument** was built to remember what happened and the people who died.
Know that a monument is something that is built to remember an important event.
Know the nursery rhyme 'London's Burning' by heart.
Extended written response: at the end of the unit, pupils will write an essay answering the question 'How did the Great Fire of London change London?'

Excerpt from year 1 history curriculum. Key vocabulary is written in bold to indicate that these words/concepts should be understood by the pupils in the context given.

Setting out the precise details of the curriculum in the smallest possible units of knowledge ensures that key vocabulary and concepts can be revisited time and time again in a multitude of contexts to embed learning. If we discover that an essential building block is missing later on, it becomes possible to add this key knowledge in to previous year groups. For example, it came to light that a number of our year 5 pupils had only heard the word 'party' in the context of celebrations and had little understanding of the term used to signify, for example, a political party. This led to great confusion when discussing current affairs relating to a general election with visions of party leaders wearing brightly coloured hats and excitedly playing pass the parcel. With a curriculum set out in such detail, it was possible to include explicit reference to political parties when our year 2 pupils learn about Barack Obama as the first black president of America and when our year 3 pupils compare democracy in Ancient Greece with modern democracy in the UK.

Knowledge is acquired in long-term memory

Whilst we endeavoured to curate a rich curriculum, we were aware that all of our efforts would be in vain if the curriculum itself was not remembered by pupils. What use is knowing about the states of matter in year 4 if pupils can't remember it in year 5 when they learn about reversible changes such as dissolving? The curriculum must then be structured in a way that makes schema development unavoidable. As Dylan Wiliam states, 'The main purpose of curriculum is to build up the content of long-term memory so that when students are asked to think, they are able to think in more powerful ways because what is in their long-term memories makes their short-term memories more powerful. That is why curriculum matters' (Wiliam, 2018). If children remember what they have learnt about the causes of the Great Fire of London, for example, this will enable them to think more powerfully about likely causes of forest fires or why fires are more common in Brazilian favelas. They will be more able to think about how towns should be planned and buildings constructed to prevent fire spreading and will be able to transfer learning in one context to other, quite different contexts.

The work of Nick Soderstrom and Robert Bjork on the distinction between learning and performance was instructive in helping us to recognise that pupils can often perform well in lessons and that this gives the illusion of learning. As they state in their paper 'Learning versus Performance: An Integrative Review': 'The distinction between learning and performance is crucial because there now exists overwhelming empirical evidence showing that considerable learning can occur in the absence of any performance gains and, conversely, that substantial changes in performance often fail to translate into corresponding changes in learning' (Soderstrom and Bjork, 2015).

When we began to consider the implications of this distinction, we realised that we needed to invest time in ensuring content was secured in long-term memory and to be cautious about making judgements about learning from performance in lessons. How would we go about ensuring that learning resulted in permanent changes in long-term memory?

One of the most well-established findings from cognitive science is the effect often known as the testing effect or retrieval effect. The finding, first detailed in the seminal study by Edwin Abbott in 1909, has been replicated many times across a range of contexts including recently in history facts (Carpenter et al., 2009), foreign languages (Pyc and Rawson, 2010) and statistics (Lyle and Crawford, 2011). The central finding is that long-term memory is enhanced when time is devoted to retrieving information that is to be remembered in the future. In other words, the act of recalling what we know strengthens the memory for that information. We soon realised that when the curriculum was poorly defined, opportunities for retrieval practice became difficult and too imprecise to have the greatest impact. While teachers might be able to quiz pupils on what they themselves have taught, it was difficult to retrieve anything from previous year groups as the precise details of the curriculum were nebulous. With a curriculum set out in such detail we can now ask more pertinent questions to enable retrieval of previously learned information. Instead of just asking generic open-ended questions such as 'What do you remember about last year's work on Vikings?', we can also now probe more precisely asking 'What was the first recorded Viking raid?', 'Why did they attack Lindisfarne?', 'What was the significance of this raid?' and 'Why was the *Anglo-Saxon Chronicle* important to historians studying these events?'

Knowledge is carefully sequenced over time

The careful sequencing of a curriculum takes a great deal of thought, but without this we run the risk of leaving pupils with gaps in understanding as they tackle more challenging work moving through school. Concepts and contexts are introduced in the early years and revisited over time to facilitate retention in long-term memory, building on the background knowledge secured earlier. As Christine Counsell eloquently describes: 'Curriculum is content structured as narrative over time' (Counsell, 2018). As we looked afresh at our curriculum, we asked ourselves questions such as 'After seven years in school, what should our pupils know and understand of this particular subject?' and 'How is knowledge organised in the curriculum to ensure pupils have the required prior knowledge to progress quickly?'

When our reception children listen to the story of 'The Emperor's New Clothes', they begin to develop a tentative understanding of the concept of 'empire' in history. This concept then develops further during a study of the extent of the Roman Empire in year 3 and culminates with a local history study into Oldham's place in the Industrial Revolution where we examine the British Empire under Queen Victoria. Repeated exposure to the concept using different contexts provides pupils with a nuanced and multifaceted view of the subject.

Our year 1 history unit on the Great Fire of London (see p, 77) introduces a number of key concepts that are woven like threads throughout the history curriculum.

These include:

1. Source
   The concept of a source is explored through the initial discussion as the place where the fire began. Later the word 'source' is used to describe how Pepys's diary helps us to learn about the events of the past. In subsequent years, pupils study other sources of evidence such as Martin Luther King's 'Letter from a Birmingham Jail' while studying civil rights and Anne Frank's diary when learning about Jewish persecution in the 1940s.

2. Monarchy
   This is the first instance of the concept of monarchy in the curriculum. Later on, in year 2, pupils study the current royal family and understand that a hereditary monarchy is one in which the crown is passed down from one member of the royal family to the next. In year 3, they examine how the Roman Republic differed from the system of monarchy; and then, in year 5, they study the Preclassic Mayan civilisation and learn how a ruler can have unlimited autocratic power in an absolute monarchy. In this way, the concept of monarchy is developed explicitly over time, taking in multiple perspectives.

3. Cause and consequence
   Causal explanation is a prominent aspect of history teaching which is accessible to young children. This unit explores how the hot summer preceding the fire, the construction of the houses in close proximity to each other and the materials used for construction all exacerbated

the fire. Pupils learn that the London Fire Brigade was founded as a consequence of the fire's destruction. Each history unit in the curriculum develops the idea of cause and consequence further as a way into disciplinary thinking in history. This, in turn, will support more advanced work at key stage 3 when pupils practise historical argument in an increasingly nuanced way.

With each piece of knowledge in our curriculum earning its place as an essential building block for future learning, we aim to build a rich understanding of the world for our pupils that prepares them for the next stage of education.

Knowledge is organised into clearly defined subject disciplines

After agreeing the five principles for curriculum development, we began to contemplate the core purpose of each subject area. After years of cross-curricular thinking and a de-emphasis on foundation subjects, our understanding of the essence of each subject had become watered down. If children made something that looked good, we called it art; if it looked a mess, we called it design and technology. We agreed with HMCI Amanda Spielman when she stated that 'the conversation about curriculum and pedagogy has often been too generic. We have occasionally lost sight of the crucial differences between the subjects we teach, their long and proud history as academic disciplines, and the implications that has for the curriculum and teaching' (Spielman, 2019).

To help clarify our thinking, we turned back to the purpose of study and aims as set out in the national curriculum, which we had neglected in our rush to discover the content of the curriculum when it was first published. These gave us the basis to delve deeper into individual subject areas through joining subject associations and making links with secondary specialists. Developing subject knowledge amongst staff became a significant consideration and, as a result, we replaced a scheduled meeting each half term with self-directed study time. This enables staff to read more widely and pursue learning directly relevant to their upcoming curriculum content.

Subjects that had previously been neglected are now coming back to the fore and flourishing. Design and technology was one such 'Cinderella' subject in which projects were decided upon because of a tenuous link with whatever subject matter was being studied in the humanities curriculum. Learning about volcanoes in geography meant constructing a papier-mâché model of Mount

Etna; studying Ancient Egypt in history prompted the building of a model shadoof; and when investigating the Roman Empire, a cardboard Roman shield was the order of the day. Little was done to consider the sequence of design and technology teaching over time, and, as such, it was left to languish as an add-on to whatever curriculum content was covered elsewhere. Joining the Design and Technology Association and reading their guidance transformed our understanding of the subject. We now have a discrete curriculum for design and technology which ensures pupils develop knowledge and skills in a coherent way over time and is not beholden to the content of the humanities curriculum.

Having a better understanding of what drives, as Christine Counsell describes, 'the distinctive pursuit of truth' (2018) in each discipline has enabled us to structure a curriculum in a way that treats subject disciplines with respect, which then profoundly influences teachers' decisions about the implementation of the curriculum.

It is certainly true that building a curriculum in this way is a significant undertaking, but the fruits of this labour are indeed sweet and fulfilling. Pupils know more, remember more and can do more with what they know. With a well-structured curriculum built upon prior knowledge secured in long-term memory, we are building a sturdier foundation for our pupils, ensuring they are dealt a good hand to provide them with the best possible start in life.

References

Abbott, E.E. (1909) 'On the analysis of the factor of recall in the learning process', *Psychological Monographs: General and Applied* 11 (1) pp 159–177.

Carpenter, S. K., Pashler, H. and Cepeda, N. J. (2009) 'Using tests to enhance 8th grade students' retention of US history facts', *Applied Cognitive Psychology* 23 (6) pp. 760–771.

Counsell, C. (2018) 'Taking curriculum seriously', *Impact* 4. Retrieved from www.bit.ly/38MXnZJ

Didau, D. (2015) 'The problem with lesson planning', *Learning Spy* [Blog]. Retrieved from www.bit.ly/3bdDKMd

Hirsch, E. D. (2016) *Why knowledge matters: rescuing our children from failed educational theories.* Cambridge, MA: Harvard Education Press.

Lyle, K. B. and Crawford N. A. (2011) 'Retrieving essential material at the end of lectures improves performance on statistics exams', *Teaching of Psychology* 38 (2) pp. 94–97.

Pyc, M. A. and Rawson, K. A. (2010) 'Why testing improves memory: mediator effectiveness hypothesis', *Science* 330 (6002) p. 335.

Rosenshine, B. (2012) 'Principles of instruction: research-based strategies that all teachers should know', *American Educator* 36 (1) pp. 12–19, 39

Shing, Y. L. and Brod, G. (2016) 'Effects of prior knowledge on memory: implications for education', *Mind, Brain, and Education* 10 (3) pp. 153–161.

Soderstrom, N. C. and Bjork, R. A. (2015) 'Learning versus performance: an integrative review', *Perspectives on Psychological Science* 10 (2) pp. 176–199.

Spielman, A. (2019) *Speech at the 2019 ASCL annual conference.* 16 March. Retrieved from www.bit.ly/2WquIqV.

Wiliam, D. (2018) *Creating the schools our children need: why what we're doing now won't help much (and what we can do instead).* West Palm Beach, FL: Learning Sciences International.

Author bio-sketch:

Andrew Percival is deputy headteacher at Stanley Road Primary School in Oldham, Greater Manchester. He has been teaching and leading in schools for the past 22 years and currently leads on curriculum development and English across school. He blogs and tweets as @primarypercival.

ON WRITING A KNOWLEDGE-DRIVEN ENGLISH CURRICULUM

DOUG LEMOV AND EMILY BADILLO

A few years ago, we started to re-imagine reading instruction, but the thought of writing a curriculum never entered our minds. There were things we thought reading teachers could do differently (some of which Doug described in his 2016 book written with Colleen Driggs and Erica Woolway, *Reading Reconsidered*), but we thought it would work to simply make the case to teachers directly. If we explained useful ideas and our case was convincing, teachers would apply the ideas, each in their own unique way, and better teaching would spread and evolve.

It turned out it wasn't that simple.

Being knowledge-driven was a good example of 'something we thought teachers could do differently'. Let's say a class was reading *Number the Stars*, Lois Lowry's novel set during the Nazi occupation of Copenhagen in 1943. A teacher who provided background knowledge on topics like the rationing of goods such as sugar and butter would help students to better comprehend key passages, like the one where the protagonist, Annemarie, scoffs dismissively at her little sister's desire for a pink frosted cupcake. Understanding how rationing affected characters they had come to care about would cause students to comprehend the book more deeply and glean more knowledge for next time through their reading. They would come to understand both the psychology of rationing – the childish fixations of a younger sibling; the snappish responses of an older one – as much as the logistics – long-lines; distribution schedules; black market goods. They could apply this knowledge to other contexts in their future studies. Students would understand the text more deeply, in other words; but with the right reflections in the course of reading, they would also increase their knowledge far more quickly for next time. Add a dozen short articles on, say, resistance movements, how small children understand complex realities or how occupying armies interact with civilians, and suddenly not only would the book be a richer read, it could become a knowledge-generating machine. The knowledge might seem at first unique to the book's setting but facts, understood deeply, don't stay disconnected for long.

There were other things we believed about improving the teaching of English. For example:

- Students should be comfortable with challenging texts and the idea of struggle. This would be one of the fundamental experiences of their lives at university and as professionals. They should have tools they use to attend to and unpack the written word when it proves complex. Proficiency with such tools can be improved through steady exposure and deliberate practice.
- Reading a book should be a writing-intensive experience, and that writing should be a tool students use not just to express and justify existing opinions, but to discover what they think in the first place. And students should be taught to expand their syntactic control – their mastery of tools to help them write sentences that capture nuanced and sophisticated ideas – in a methodical way.
- Reading a book is a social phenomenon. Reading a book together as a class means everyone laughing or gasping, together in a room, hearing and coming to understand both shared experience and how others may have viewed it differently. The power of this shared experience was a primary reason for the rise of written language as a source of enjoyment and wisdom rather than the mere transfer of technical information. Good classrooms could recreate that feeling of deeply shared experience. Perhaps if books are to survive in the age of the smartphone, they must.
- Vocabulary is the single most important form of background knowledge and teaching it well requires constant opportunities to use and play with words in different settings, so good vocabulary instruction should start with, rather than end at, the definition.

Useful ideas, we hope, but even when teachers agreed with them, they struggled to implement them into their teaching. They weren't able to go home and source short non-fiction passages about resistance movements in wartime, for example. Who knew where to find such an article; and once you found it, it needed editing – there were long digressions about less relevant topics, or part of the key information was in one article and part of it was in another. It took time teachers didn't have, especially when preparing lessons after making dinner and just possibly putting their own children to bed.

Developing just the right writing prompts or the text-dependent questions that would allow for successful close reading of challenging books took time as well – more time than people teaching four preps and grading 150 papers had available on their lunch break when they were – *whoops!* – also supposed to be covering the lunch room. And it took expertise. Your 150th close-reading question is better than your 3rd, we have since discovered, especially when a team of colleagues gives you regular feedback on them.

Teachers rarely take courses in instructional design, Robert Pondiscio pointed out in a recent commentary (2016). It's a completely different skill from teaching a lesson, but one we assume teachers will naturally be able to do well. 'It's like expecting the waiter at your favorite restaurant to serve your meal attentively while simultaneously cooking for twenty-five other people – and doing all the shopping and prepping the night before. You'd be exhausted too,' Pondiscio writes.

Elsewhere, Pondiscio points out that around 90% of English teachers find their lesson content by googling – sometimes desperately – things like 'number the stars lesson ideas' the night before. 'Countless hours spent finding or creating lesson materials from scratch' (Pondiscio, 2016) could be better spent in intellectual preparation, he observes: rereading the novel, reviewing student work, or preparing to teach. Teachers were asked to do two jobs: prepare great lessons and teach them. While many teachers value (and even enjoy) the intellectual work of bringing beloved novels to life for their students, the practical demands of the job often make the quiet, contemplative hours needed to do justice to that process hard to find – especially when they are required almost daily.

It took us a long time to discover the wisdom in what Pondiscio was saying. Just because teachers believed in an idea didn't make it feasible for them to do it. And just doing it didn't guarantee anything about succeeding at it. We spent a lot of time talking about what kept teachers from having the lessons they wanted. Finally there was a meeting where someone said, 'I'm just not sure there's any way to do this without writing an actual curriculum with daily lesson plans and the like.'

After that, the room went absolutely silent.

One of the reasons the room went silent was that we'd seen a lot of the curriculums English teachers were being given – even in schools we loved and respected. Curriculum was *done to* teachers; it told them what to say and discouraged their own decision-making and precluded their own interests. Plans were unwieldy, dense documents, precisely scripted to make sure the teacher didn't say the wrong thing. Emily had a colleague who burst into her room one morning, marked-up lesson plan in her hand. Twenty-two years old and desperate to do right by her students, she had spent hours memorizing the detailed lesson plan provided by the network. Like an actor's script, her lesson plan was highlighted, annotated, dogeared. But her copy of the novel was blank. She was so busy trying to remember what she was supposed to say, she hadn't had time to finish (or think much about) the book yet. How would she react when a student asked her something unexpected about a character or idea?

We wanted a curriculum that loved books and teachers, that supported them and could respond to where they were in their own teaching journey: question by question for a new teacher, with suitable autonomy and flexibility for a master. There had to be a way to help teachers without giving them a straitjacket. We were imagining something that gave teachers great lessons to use and that respected their knowledge even while supplementing it. If we wanted to help teachers approach teaching English differently, we'd have to make it so they were happy with the trade.

One of the ways we tried to do that was to rely on teachers like Emily as designers – people who had experienced a variety of approaches and would always see the lesson through the eyes of someone who had to stand up in front of 30 young people and bring it to life.

When Emily first started teaching, she remembers, her students often did everything she asked of them, but her classes still felt all wrong. Her pupils diligently annotated the texts they read and crafted written responses, memorizing five types of character inferences and eight steps to find the main idea. Anchor charts papered the walls; chants echoed down the hallway. Each of her lessons was organized around one transferable skill. The class would master it, and then (she hoped) they'd forever be able to infer a character's motivation from their actions, dialogue, and thoughts. Over and over, text after text, they'd find a handy character and chart the relevant evidence, then dutifully slot the evidence into the rigid format of a paragraph response.

In discussion, Emily was taught to use a prompting guide, a spiral-bound document of questions aligned to each reading skill. The ideal discussion was one in which teachers asked no 'text-specific' questions, the thinking being that universal prompts would be more broadly applicable to future texts. As student discussion veered off course, Emily would find herself flipping through the prompting guide, trying to diagnose the skill gap and find the perfect question to bring students back on track without asking about specific characters or plot points. In the midst of this process, the novel seemed to die. She and her students talked about the prompt and the evidence needed to answer it, but less often the book itself.

Their writing was just as troubling. It was painful to read. Tortured syntax, ideas crammed into strict frames supplemented by carefully copied but completely irrelevant evidence from the text.

The moments in class that felt electric were often accidental. One day, Emily and her students were reading the novel *Chains,* a beautifully written but challenging work of historical fiction set in 18th-century colonial America. In one scene, a servant attempts to explain the dynamics of the household to the protagonist, a young enslaved girl. About the master's widowed aunt, the servant explains:

> She's old and rich, and owns land in three countries. The master hopes to inherit the lot when she dies, so they treat her like the Queen herself. To her face at least.

In their written responses, students had been struggling to make inferences about character motivation; asking, 'What does the character want or need?' led to blank stares. Out of ideas, Emily remembers closing the prompting guide and rereading the scene as a group, pausing to define the word 'inherit' and explaining whom the phrase 'the Queen' alluded to. The resulting discussion was enthusiastic, accurate, and even fun. Students were able to live in the text in a different, richer way when they weren't trying to force each scene into a tidy formula of Motivation + Obstacle = Conflict.

Curious about other approaches to teaching reading, Emily switched schools and, ironically, went from one flawed model to its opposite.

She began teaching at an arts-based, progressive charter school in Manhattan with a less structured approach to reading that she hoped would be more effective for students (and more sustainable for herself). The model was student-led and self-directed. The ideal lesson started on the carpet with Emily in the middle, occasionally reading aloud to students, who then created projects in groups based on the stories. While this model preserved the joy of reading and freed teachers and students from the pressure to support every argument with three pieces of evidence from the text, the emphasis on group work and self-directed learning had other costs.

The model valorized choice reading. Every week ended with 'Library Friday', an entire class period in which students read books of their choice, snuggled into bean bag chairs in the corner of the classroom. The thinking was that each child knows best what interests them, so students should be most motivated to read if they pursue their passions and select their own books. But it was hard to tell how much and how well each of 25 children was reading. And the model was strangely isolating. No one ever changed their opinion about a book because a classmate pushed them to see it differently. Kids rarely read something that they didn't think they'd like at first but that moved and inspired them. It was a bit of an echo chamber; a monument to the idea that as long as kids were reading something, all was well. The students who already loved reading adored this time, devouring book after book. But for the students who didn't love to read, or were easily distracted, or who struggled to read attentively, or who did not read on grade level but were embarrassed to choose easier texts, it was 60 minutes of idly flipping pages.

And project-based learning was fun, but was it teaching students to read deeply? Had a student really grappled with *Island of the Blue Dolphins*, for example, if their major project was to make their own version of Karana's skirt out of paper feathers? Without a grounding in historical context to help them understand early contacts between native peoples and traders, without independent writing that caused them to think about loneliness and isolation, without a closer look at Karana's decisions at the end of the book – the two marks she makes on her face, her acceptance of the western dress her rescuers make for her to wear – it was hard to say that students had fully read it.

The truth was, students had to write frequently to understand a text – and to be able to feel its full emotional resonance. They had to be able to unpack a thorny patch of resistant text instead of skipping over it. They got more things, unexpected things, out of shared reading but they had to learn to listen carefully during discussions. And hands-on experiences like role-playing or debating what a character should have done in a crucial scene were a lot more beneficial when they were grounded in knowledge (and therefore reality), so students weren't guessing, often erroneously, about life in the 19th century. 'I'd tell them to go away,' wasn't an especially useful response to the arrival of the Russian traders in the opening scenes of *Island of the Blue Dolphins*, no matter how heartfelt. In other words, a funny thing happened when Emily started to design more rigorous and demanding activities for her students while also giving them knowledge to support their understanding: they liked reading more. A lot of the activities designed to motivate and engage students had the perverse effect of replacing the core act of reading. But there were moments that proved that reading, done differently, could be just as engaging and motivating as making posters or acting out key scenes.

Our first step was to build a model – a unit that tested all of the elements we wanted to include. For this, we used the book *Esperanza Rising*, a novel set equally in Mexico and California describing the journey of the daughter of a once wealthy rancher killed and dispossessed in the aftermath of the Mexican revolution as she migrates to the United States. It took us six tries to get our 'knowledge organizer' – a summary of key background knowledge students would need to get the most out of the book – right. We included historical readings about the Mexican caste system. We included a study of Dorothea Lange's photographs to understand the plight of the Okies who arrive later in the book but refined and tweaked the questions to create a wider range of writing experiences (e.g. 'Write a page from Lange's journal from the day she took this photo'). In asking students to unlock the symbolism of the produce for which chapters were named – figs, onions, roses – we provided background on how each was often used: people often referred to the layers of an onion, or to the fact that they made one cry in chopping them, or to the fact that onions were simple and cheap, often peasant fare. Did one of these meanings apply? Or something different.

Once our unit was built, we tried it out in the classrooms of four or five willing teachers. We observed and solicited feedback. They loved the vocabulary; the pacing was challenging. We guest-taught some lessons ourselves and then made changes, especially changes that teachers said would make the lessons easier to use. We developed support materials: an overview and a unit plan for each book; a curriculum guide to explain all the parts of the lessons; and we shot videos of quality implementation to show what ten minutes of vocabulary or close reading should look like so teachers could see and study models.

Our curriculum was always designed to be built around books – exploring and unpacking their layers, hearing the increasingly familiar mannerisms of an author's voice and persistent echoes of a time period, getting the jokes and perceiving the subtle hints. These experiences form a relationship between students and books that shorter forms of text cannot replicate. It makes books an irreplaceable part of one's schooling. Books get inside us and stay there. What's more, the books themselves matter. Books like *Animal Farm* and *Narrative of the Life of Frederick Douglass* matter, not just because people will allude to them at university, but because of the way deeply reading a book can change who you are. To 'pass over' into the mind of another person, to understand their perspective intellectually and emotionally, is to live part of their experience and to 'return enlarged', the scientist and philosopher of reading Maryanne Wolf writes (2018).

With that in mind, we set out to choose the books. (Our curriculum has poetry and short story units, but these are designed to be 'book length', i.e. about six weeks in duration.) We thought a typical teacher could teach five or six books really well in a year – in a way that modeled what it meant to become immersed in a text, that is. That meant that a book was a scarce and precious resource. Each choice had to be of immensely high quality. But what were the right six books, the ones that let students read books of historical significance but that also represented a diversity of perspectives? Were the right six books for 30 seventh graders in Dallas the same as those for seventh graders in New York or Fresno – or Liverpool for that matter? Or for two teachers right down the hall from one another in Dallas but with different interests and passions? How could we balance the benefits of choice with the benefits of shared knowledge – the idea that if you wanted to make connections across texts, you couldn't get very far unless there were books you could reliably assume all of your students had read. We called this an 'internal canon': each school needed a balanced selection of shared books that everyone had read and could talk about. We looked for books that were diverse, challenging, important, and inspiring. Books that gave rise to rich conversations about knowledge and that were challenging enough that students could take on the best the English language had to offer without fear. And books that, brought to life in the classroom, would be unforgettable. We decided early on to make the curriculum 'modular' to give schools and teachers an array of books to choose from and let them each choose their ideal six. The right decision in one school need not be the right decision in another.

Our design process is simple but, some might say, backwards. We start each lesson as an adult reader, rereading the day's section of the book. What's happening on the page? What moments in the text make us sit up a little straighter, reach for that highlighter, raise our eyebrows? Where is the language doing something interesting? Then, we interrogate those responses – what tiny choices, what turns of phrase, what buildups of tension made that moment happen? Why this word and not another? How can we break down the layers of nuance and connection that created our experience as adult readers, and, through a series of questions, guide a room of 12-year-olds to a similar insight?

This process might sound obvious but the core idea – that the objective for each lesson starts with and is driven by the book – is the opposite of what many curricula do. They start with a learning standard and attempt to make the book support that goal. Over time, we felt, this risks losing touch with the reason one is reading the book in the first place. We wanted to let the book guide us, to write a curriculum by and for people who love books, meant to create more people who love books.

In our curriculum, we draw on technical literary vocabulary: passive voice, alliteration, intrusive narration. We dive deeply into historical context: what would a student need to know about the life of a Victorian-era London cab driver to understand this scene in *The Magician's Nephew*? What makes a boarding school uniform so significant in *Lord of the Flies*? (And for that matter, what is a boarding school uniform? Or even a boarding school?) We track down obscure allusions and references, looking for that grain of context that snaps meaning into place: a text on spiritual chanting to help students understand the power of the community's chant in *The Giver*, an article on dissociation and trauma to make sense of fragmented narration in *Freak the Mighty*.

It isn't easy, and we're still figuring it out, but we believe in planning this way because this process – notice, wonder, dig deeper, step back – brings a text to life. We strive for balance: open to an emotional experience but grounded in knowledge. Digging into the granular, word-by-word choices an author makes, while remaining connected to other moments within and across books. Sharing a text with the class but grappling in writing on our own.

This planning process takes time, but it saves time for teachers – an observation that highlights the difference between lessons planning (the process described above) and lesson preparation (the process of getting ready to teach a lesson no matter who has written it). We believe that time spent in preparation is the most valuable a teacher can spend. Great close-reading questions only truly work with a teacher who has considered which students she'll ask which questions of, who will read each section, and what additional questions she'll ask when students struggle. We're happy to research and write an article on the role of the planet Venus in science fiction if that means a teacher has more time to read student writing about Ray Bradbury.

We imagine that the accumulation of units taught in this way will create the bank of knowledge students need in high school and beyond. And then an allusion in *Lord of the Flies* reminds you of an allusion you read in *The*

93

Magician's Nephew years earlier. The feeling of reading a dense, thorny text that resists you, that makes no sense, and then gradually peeling back the layers to find a truth or nuance you would have missed – that doesn't leave you. Even being able to recognize and name: this is an allusion to something I don't understand yet. The author is using a metaphor here but I'm not sure why. Imagine how approaching reading in this way can change the narrative for students. What power in being able to shift from 'I'm not a good reader' to 'I don't know about this yet'. From 'I can't make inferences' to 'What do I need to learn more about?' The mental process of establishing meaning first, then shifting to analysis is replicable across units and years. Normalizing rereading, valorizing research, but above all, putting the book back at the centre of class.

Because in our curriculum, the book is the thing – not the objectives and standards and skills and terms surrounding it. If you're reading with a teacher who breathes life into the text, if you take the time to read closely and someone helps you build knowledge of the parts that are unfamiliar, we believe you will end the unit a stronger reader than when you began it, more attuned to the subtle choices authors make, and better able to live in the next book you open.

References

Pondiscio, R. (2016) 'Failing by design: how we make teaching too hard for mere mortals', *The Thomas B. Fordham Institute* [Website], 10 May. Retrieved from: www.bit.ly/34B8HaW

Wolf, M. (2018) 'What does immersing yourself in a book do to your brain?', *Literary Hub* [Website], 8 August. Retrieved from: www.bit.ly/2ygbTNf

Author bio-sketches:
Emily Badillo received a bachelor's degree in English from Stanford University and a master's degree in education from Hunter College. She has eight years of experience teaching middle and elementary schools students in New York City, and joined the Teach Like a Champion team in 2018. She is currently one of the writers working on TLAC's reading curriculum.

Doug Lemov is the author of *Teach Like a Champion* (now in its 2.0 version), *Practice Perfect* and *Reading Reconsidered*. He's a former English teacher and school leader and is now the managing director of a team at Uncommon Schools that provides professional development and curriculum tools for schools.

BETTER CONVERSATIONS WITH SUBJECT LEADERS

HOW SECONDARY SENIOR LEADERS CAN SEE A CURRICULUM MORE CLEARLY

CHRISTINE COUNSELL

Introduction

As the final phase of a general education before specialisation kicks in, pre-16 secondary education gives school leaders a peculiar challenge. Secondary education requires specialist subject teachers yet stays, for the last time in compulsory schooling, dauntingly broad in scope. The net effect of this conjunction of depth and breadth is that senior leaders' subject knowledge is outstripped by that of the teachers. Yet a senior leadership team (SLT) is accountable for these knowledge goods – their choice, their quality, their journey and their effectiveness in transforming pupils.

These knowledge goods are the object of learning – the thing being learned. Their curricular realisation – through scoping, shaping and patterning according to subject rhythms – is of profound importance. Curriculum is the means by which we ensure that knowledge does its work of transformation. Pupils' knowledge of specific history, music or science will alter what they can notice, analyse or enjoy in subsequent material. New fluency in language or number generates memory space, stamina or curiosity for more complex operations.

When the substance of education itself – its object, the thing being learned – is even partly concealed from senior leaders, those leaders must ascertain its quality through proxies, such as the proxy of assessment and results or the proxy of general teaching quality. But therein lie the dangers. Proxies designed to give information about pupils' progress may mislead. Senior and middle leaders commonly discuss *which* pupils are learning, but such monitoring can be meaningless without attention to *what* pupils are learning.

SLT must take assurance from middle leaders, but how?

One solution to all this is simply to trust subject leaders, to create conditions for their flourishing and to get out of the way. Where strong departments are autonomously self-improving, this, as Fordham (2020a) argues, is nirvana. But to state that aspiration may be to oversimplify the challenge, and for three reasons. First, such happy situations are far from universal. Senior leaders need to gauge where a department is on its journey and to know what is and isn't helping. Second, even where departments work optimally and provide superb education, the senior leader needs to know *what* is working well, and *why*. They will neither understand the significance of pupils' achievement en route, nor grasp the features of professional development that make the difference, nor speak meaningfully about what the school does well, if the essence of this subject brilliance is opaque. Third, a school must be run as a coherent enterprise. Subjects must, in certain spheres, be transcended. School leaders must allocate resource fairly, consider time relative to productivity, facilitate collaboration, align systems, review progress across spheres, define effectiveness and create environments conducive to learning. They need to know enough to ensure that any whole-school policies make it easier, not harder, for good subject teachers to thrive and for subjects to be taught well.

So what kind of SLT understanding is possible and how can it be achieved? At this point, we could slide into an impractical game of specifying what SLT need to know about each subject in order to avoid the above dangers. This chapter tackles the problem differently, focusing instead on questions SLT can ask so as to reveal opportunities and pitfalls. SLT need to stay vigilant that management practices are illuminating, rather than concealing, what the curriculum content is *doing* – in intent and reality – to change pupils.

In this chapter, I first elaborate dangers of common proxies. I then suggest six ways in which leaders can interrogate subjects and subject curricula outside their own specialism. Finally, I illustrate curricular conversations in three management settings.

How proxies conceal the curriculum, and therefore everything else

First, the proxy of results. What do exam results tell us about the quality of a curriculum?

Some curriculum aims are relatively straightforward. If our aim is basic literacy or numeracy, a test result might show that a curriculum was effective in achieving said aim. But what is 'effectiveness' in secondary history, music or literature curricula? Reduce it to a threshold of results improvement and we confuse measure of outcome with real outcome. If a big hike in progress sees 75% of pupils finally securing grade 4 in GCSE English Literature, this may tell us little about quality of curriculum because a '4' represents a very low baseline indeed, and will be a sign neither that pupils read widely or independently, nor that they write critically and creatively. A qualification may have been scraped by rehearsal of formulae based on extracts, a travesty of English itself, and violence may have been done to love of literature. Moreover, if 25% of pupils cannot even achieve this low level, the efficacy of reducing the curriculum to surface examination skills must be questioned. What have these students, and those who scraped a '4', *not* experienced, earlier in their curriculum, which might have changed them in more substantial and sustainable ways? Meanwhile, 75% securing a '4' or above in an optional subject such as French or history may distract from the important question of why (say) 50% (or far fewer) were deemed capable of continuing these subjects into the examination years.

To fail to prioritise such questions is to fail to place the lower-school curriculum within a theory of improvement. Only serious attention to underlying components from year 7 is going to bring about substantial and sustainable change.

A second proxy is the use of assessment and data en route. This can stand in for discussion about *what* has been learned and its role in making future progress possible. This problem was at its most prevalent when schools based internal assessment on ladders of skill hierarchy, whether England's 'level descriptions' from a former national curriculum, reinventions of these (such as 'emerging', 'demonstrating', 'extending') or examination mark schemes. Relying on any of these as progression models masks the role of the entire content substance in actually changing the pupils. It fails to treat *the curriculum itself* as the progression model. SLT-MLT conversation about data must reveal what year 8 know about biomes, the stereotyping of Brazilian *favelas* or resource management in the Amazon basin, and how these content choices enable pupils to grasp *new* geographical content or tackle the next challenge of geographical thinking.

A third proxy occurs when application of cognitive science is called 'curriculum'. I often hear teachers claiming an evidence-based approach to curriculum with reference to science of memory such as cognitive load theory (Kirschner, 2002) or resulting practical precepts (e.g. Rosenshine, 2012). Retrieval, deliberate practice, spaced practice and overlearning can certainly be built into curriculum flow in support of efficient learning but they do not get us close to subject curriculum matters such as the infinite, contested content of literature, history or music and its infinite configurations. Moreover, if senior leaders look for application of cognitive science in classrooms without attention to *what* is singled out for recall or rehearsal, then, at best, curriculum itself is concealed from view. At worst, the entity being recalled may be poorly chosen, privileging the wrong detail, interrupting narrative flow or destroying the shaping of content that makes it memorable.

In the crowded territory of a subject's complex content, the question of *what* is recalled is not a given. Well-spaced retrieval is not curricular thinking. Its presence tells us little about rigour and scope of component choice, how a subject's forms of accounting shape content and create meaning, or how pupils come to see those accounts as authored and purposeful.

The problem with these three proxies being used as means and measure of improvement is that the efficacy of the means or the value of the measure depends on the quality of curriculum that the proxy mediates. Neither exam results, nor interim data, nor cognitive psychology tells us about whether the resulting knowledge goods are worth having or whether the curriculum journey towards them worked optimally. Furthermore, these things may have done damage. Whole-school teaching policies or uncritical assumptions about the value of qualifications may constrain subject teaching or distort subject properties as teachers have often narrated (e.g. Walker, 2018).

Getting beyond proxies to subject difference: an example from chemistry and history

Compare the following two scenarios in which the opening episode of a lesson involves retrieving prior knowledge.

Year 10 chemistry are working on ionic compounds. In preparation for new work on ionic structures, pupils must recall their earlier work on ionic bonding. Pupils work systematically through exercises that foster this retrieval, thereby reinforcing and using prior learning. Retrieval is visibly construed as practice: pupils apply a very particular and stable thing, repeatedly, in varied contexts.

Year 10 history are working on modern American history. They are preparing to produce arguments in response to a question about whether USA liberal democracy has ever been under threat. They need confidence with the ever-slippery term 'liberal' and readily available comparators of democracies which might be judged fragile or secure. Their teacher now asks them to recall year 8 work on 19th-century Germany and Italy (how liberalism and nationalism arose hand in hand), year 9 work on democracy giving way to authoritarianism in Weimar Germany and year 8 work on democracy's fortunes waxing and waning in 19th-century Britain. Pupils use all this to advance ideas on how to characterise the state of liberal democracy at particular moments in US history. Unprompted, some pupils also draw on recent work on decolonisation.

At first sight, these two examples of strong curriculum planning are similar. Previously taught components become functional in enabling pupils to assimilate new material and do worthwhile things with it. Because the new work *necessitates* the retrieval, the retrieval finds a natural home within it. Thinner KS3 history curricula, with no 19th-century Europe, would slow down discussion of the term 'liberal' and limit comparisons useful for spotting the significance of twists in US narratives. Weaker KS3 science curricula would see pupils unable to progress this far in chemistry because prior components had not been practised to security.

So far, so similar.

Or actually not so similar. The two recaps are different:

- I would not call the history example 'practice' because the term implies an isolation of the conceptual layer from its narrative moorings.
- What pupils recall from earlier work in chemistry is complex, wide-ranging, precise, essential and non-negotiable. What pupils recall in history is complex, wide-ranging, precise and cumulatively sufficient: collectively, the prior history is critical to the students' new success, but replace certain details with equivalents and the students may do as well.
- All the recalled material in chemistry may be on the GCSE specification. It would be possible for none of the recalled history material to be on a GCSE specification. The wide sweep of reference so powerfully supportive of exam success is way beyond the scope of the exam.
- A thing called 'ionic compounds' may be on our chemistry specification, but 'liberal democracy' is not, as a universal entity, on the history specification. Rather, a chunk of American history is on the specification.

- The chemistry curriculum is a logical sequencing of regularities. The history course enshrines a paradox: concepts such as 'liberal democracy' are essential, but the curriculum is not designed around them. The concepts do a different job. They cannot live outside particular contexts. And from those contexts emerge quite other curricular considerations – from narrative shaping to the debates of scholars – which are the *main* drivers of selection and sequencing.

All this has profound implications for SLT trying to 'see' the curriculum in either subject. A failure to respect the above differences could lead to faulty readings of department or pupil achievement, or a failure to prompt a department to diagnose underlying problems. As Fordham (2020b) illustrates, auditing the mere presence of a generic teaching approach, such as retrieval practice, without 'seeing' the curriculum could prove a poor management exercise. It may mask weak curricula or, worse, if mandated in a particular form (such as types of quizzing exercise), lead to distortions that we would have been better without. The history being recalled inheres in various narrative shapes and scales: from history's stories themselves to the lesson sequence gradually revealing angles of argument. Stopping for multiple choice on definitions might be an inefficient replacement for using the narrative dynamic itself – or even a terrible idea if, say, liberal democracy were to appear as universal and fixed.

How are chemistry and history so different? 'Knowledge' might mean accounts, examples, cases, artistic works and genres or it might mean something quite different – concepts operating in laws, theories and models. A subject such as geography blends these two – the localised particulars and the systematised efforts to simplify the complex. History's powerful, shifting generalisations can certainly be interrelated; but once given status as models, we have stopped doing history. Moreover, history's stories are not mere handmaidens for illustrating a concept. Narratives matter in their own right, both to build a temporal frame of reference and to be challenged and reconfigured. Likewise, in English, texts are not studied just as illustrations of metaphor or Romanticism. The individual text matters, both as an abiding literary experience and as a reference point in intertextual webs.

Maton (2014) uses the idea of semantic gravity to weigh how far knowledge is pulled down by infinite particulars and tied to context. In science, because a few stable principles are so transferable that they explain infinite phenomena, semantic gravity is weak. History and literature, however, have much semantic gravity. While full of meanings that operate across time, place and culture, these meanings illuminate particulars rather than homogenise them; and shifting meanings themselves become objects of study.

This is why attempts in humanities curricula to theorise relationships between concepts can lead one away from a subject's concerns. The New Zealand-based Curriculum Design Coherence (CDC) tool, originally from an engineering course, was recently used to build an inferentially structured system of meaning between concepts in history teaching. The example of 'liberal democracy' was broken into the *idea* of liberal democracy ('equality', 'rights', 'nationhood'), the *operation* of liberal democracy ('government', 'legal institutions', 'social movements') and the *localisation* of liberal democracy ('tribalism', 'race', 'colony') (Rata, 2019). My concern with the CDC model applied to history is that while it helpfully theorises the relationship between abstract concepts and the materiality of content, the web of concepts itself starts to influence content selection. What we lose is history itself: its changing questions pursued by scholars, its modes of disciplinary argument, its types and standards of truth claim, its narrative framing and, above all, the traditions of history teachers which, through published curricular work, have theorised all this for specifically historical purposes.

Models applied across subjects have explanatory power but must never replace subject-sensitive precepts for subject-curriculum building which are rightly less concerned with finding a language that operates across subjects.

Six principles for interrogating curriculum to uncover subject distinctiveness

So how can SLT get close to curriculum, despite not being expert in 12 subjects? The following six principles are not ways to usurp a subject leader's role. They are, rather, principles for enabling SLT to avoid damage from generic policies, to foster departmental flourishing, and, where appropriate, to lead subject-informed debate about how to make the curriculum bigger than the sum of its parts.

Principle 1: Let each subject speak through its own, most useful curricular categories

The column headings of each subject's work schemes are critically important to get right, but there are many ways to get them wrong. A frequent request I receive from headteachers is for a whole-school planning grid. They imagine column headings such as 'knowledge', 'skills' or 'concepts'. The goal is consistency, but common headings can only achieve pretence of consistency, while also causing grief for those subjects lumbered with non-optimal headings.

As overarching categories, 'skill' ('knowing how' or 'procedural knowledge') and 'knowledge' ('knowing that' or 'propositional knowledge') can be elbowed into most subjects, somehow or other, but they are not necessarily the best high-level generalisations for the types of subject building block which cumulatively foster expertise in a subject domain. In mathematics and languages, a knowledge-skill separation makes little sense, and even in subjects where the headings 'knowledge' and 'skill' do work, they will not connote equivalence across those subjects.

Thus we arrive at the irony that a common barrier to SLT being able to understand and compare curriculum across subjects stems from a well-meaning effort to do just that – a misfired drive for consistency through common curricular categories.

Another whole-school, generic planning activity which quickly arrives at a dead end is to ask subject leaders to generate their 'most important concepts'. The result is again a set of entities with no equivalence. History teachers, for example, distinguish between second-order concepts and substantive concepts. 'Substantive concepts' just means the various nouns – abstract and concrete – that generalise about the subject's content. The term is useful in many subjects. History's substantive concepts comprise a potentially infinite list of abstract generalisations (everything from 'liberal democracy' to 'colonialism' to 'peasant'). History's 'second-order concepts' (e.g. change, continuity, causation) capture types of historical question and their resulting form of argument. They are generally used to teach history's disciplinary dimension and sometimes called 'disciplinary concepts'.

Is geography the same? Not at all. Plenty of taxonomies exist, called, variously, 'key concepts', 'big ideas' and 'organising concepts', but geographers agree neither on what they are nor on what their curricular role is (Taylor, 2008; Brooks, 2018). There is considerable international agreement that geography is concerned principally with place, space and scale, but some add others such as 'proximity and distance' (Jackson, 2006; Lambert, 2017) or 'environmental interaction' (e.g. Qualifications and Curriculum Authority, 2007). Others argue that these cannot fit into the same taxonomy as 'space and place' (Taylor, 2008). Moreover, these are complex and dynamic ideas which have evolved with the rapid development of geography as a discipline and, unlike history's 'second-order concepts', ways of operationalising them lack a tradition of collective agency from geography teachers giving them curricular traction.

Two things matter here for SLT. First, whatever high-level taxonomy geographers plump for, such concepts do not do the same job in a work scheme as history's disciplinary concepts because they do not correlate with argument structures but rather shape a certain kind of 'relational thinking' (Lambert and Morgan, 2010). You will not 'see' them working in the same way on the ground. Second, this stuff is important. Geography teachers who have thought deeply about geographical scholarship and geography education researchers are trying to show that 'thinking geographically offers a uniquely powerful way of seeing the world and making connections between scales, from the local to the global' (Jackson, 2006, p. 119).

Even if we avoid all that, and stick with 'substantive' concepts, merely having these concepts gives SLT no access to a subject's curricular logic, flow and pacing, because:

- As we saw with chemistry and history, substantive concepts, across subjects, do fundamentally different jobs in illuminating, connecting or problematising other types of material.
- Flexible familiarity with a concept is arrived at very differently and over differing timescales from one subject to another.
- In some subjects, the meaning of foundational concepts – history's 'imperialism' (Brown and Burnham, 2004), RE's 'revelation' (Kueh, 2020), music's 'tonality' (McPhail, 2017) – is expected to grow from an initial temporary coherence to being more problematised or more generative of divergence and critique. In others, secure mastery of a defined operation or factual base is the goal, and at school level at least, one is *not* aiming for it to become increasingly porous or contested.

If we abandon the constraints of common column headings, subject teams are free to think about optimal categories. Figure 1 shows four headings arrived at by three subject departments after being freed from requirements for generic headings. As we consider the headings for art and what they achieve, notice how the subject-specific terms most useful for planning necessarily become useful for SLT trying to 'read' the subjects as outsiders.[1]

---

1   The art example in figure 1 is only one way of structuring the subject. For a variation, see Stanton (2019), a pertinent example because it is written by a senior leader after conversation with the head of art.

Art			
Techniques, media and materials	The history of art, craft, design and architecture	Exploring, recording and creating	Gaining critical understanding

Modern Languages			
Grammar and syntax	Vocabulary	Phonics	Idiomatic expression

History			
Substantive content (narratives, states of affairs, periodisation, chronology)	Substantive concepts	Using second-order concepts	Understanding evidence and interpretation

Figure 1

First, note that *each* category embraces knowledge and skill. In column 1 for art, 'techniques, media and materials' comprises knowledge that pupils gain both propositionally and through practice and exploration in their own artwork. Column 2, again, would specify clear knowledge gains, strengthened by practical imitation, experimentation, comparison and reflection.

Second, it would be easy to see, at any one moment, how this art programme purposefully integrates content from across the columns. A sample moment in, say, year 8, might see the department combining a certain 'technique' (column 1) with an area of 'art history' (column 2). That nexus of choices becomes context for yet another dimension to be in play, namely 'exploring' ideas (column 3) or 'gaining critical understanding' (column 4). All curricular thinking amounts to either isolation or integration of components. Observing any moment of teaching, this is what we see – the (temporary, artificial) isolation and/or integration which makes components functional in a larger set of journeys. This furnishes SLT with useful questions such as:

- Why do you integrate X with Y?
- How does X work in conjunction with Y?
- How much practice will they need in X to complement Y?
- What are you isolating for focus here?

Third, the categories allow (or challenge) the art department to state precise increments of input, leading to discernibly cumulative reference points and proficiencies, ones that SLT can interrogate so as to find out how those curricular inputs are designed to change what pupils 'see' in their own and others' art. It allows SLT to pose the most fundamental question: what is this content *doing* here?

Fourth, we can apply useful rules of thumb at any moment: what is at stake and what is in play? All four columns will not necessarily be 'in play' in any moment. But all, always, are 'at stake', each being profoundly affected by others, over time.

Figure 1 supplies two further examples – languages and history – which illustrate the above features.

To classify or audit all this in terms of knowledge and skill would be repetitious rather than thorough. Being lean but thorough is a reason to avoid another false prophet, that of GCSE assessment objectives. GCSE assessment objectives are not a curriculum and often make poor curricular categories. A languages scheme headed by GCSE's 'four skills' of reading, writing, speaking and listening will be cumbersome in its repetition, rather than revealing the forward-projecting, foundational components that actually transform pupils' fluency and thus show the curriculum functioning as progression model (Bauckham, 2016).

At this stage, a reader might ask, but what about structural similarities across subjects? How are these to be recognised if work schemes don't itemise them?

But this *is* the job of senior leadership. Characterising pupils' net learning, discerning interdisciplinary opportunity and leading debate on how one subject serves another, is how *senior* curriculum leadership adds value. It may, indeed, be useful to know which subjects teach (say) concepts of 'evidence', 'justification' or 'proof' so that a school can establish what pupils know, overall, about epistemology. Such intellectual engagement is precisely the job of SLT. It cannot be bypassed by imposing non-optimal planning categories. To treat an illuminating theme as an audit tool is to treat curriculum as an aggregate rather than as an interlocking matrix. It replaces intellectual leadership with a superficial management device. Curriculum does not work through incidence; it works through interplay. It works across its categories and, to anticipate our next section, it works across time.

Principle 2: Interrogate how the curriculum is intended to work over time.

The question 'What is this content *doing* here?' is a powerful curriculum question for any stakeholder to ask. When given a temporal dimension, it becomes, 'How will pupils be changed such that when they *later* tackle X they will see it through new eyes?' This is to interrogate its *proximal* role in making the next bit of content understandable or some later accomplishment more secure. This might mean noticing pattern or detail, being affected by a sound world or recognising vocabulary. If a department is not thinking about what pupils can access in year 10 *as a result* of prior components, then the curriculum may as well be random aggregation.

Obvious in hierarchical subjects such as languages, mathematics and science, this principle is often acknowledged less in subjects that work only cumulatively. It matters just as much in these subjects because curriculum is knowledge structured as narrative over time. Even where there is great freedom to create the narrative, a narrative it nonetheless becomes. This is very different from asking whether one thing is more 'challenging' than another; it is about how content is positioned to obviate later, unhelpful difficulty. Our reception of the later parts of a narrative (think novel or film) are transformed by opening chapters and scenes. Prokofiev isn't intrinsically harder than Villa-Lobos. Caravaggio isn't intrinsically harder than Monet. They are as hard or easy, as boring or interesting, as prior encounter unlocks. To treat the curriculum as the progression model is to think about what effect each element may have on the pupil so that prior content joins new content to make new comparison accessible or fascinating.

Figure 2a is an English curriculum assembled by a group of heads of English. After securing adequate scope and various kinds of coherence, they reflected on sequencing and rearranged it yet again so as to optimise its workings over time. Notice how each text is carefully positioned to transform access to later texts.

Principle 3: Examine the hinterland of those subjects that require one.

We do not need to remember every word of a novel, nor the small, messy and incidental details of an historical story. But we do need to have passed through them. I recently posited the idea of a 'hinterland' (Counsell, 2018) in order to emphasise that actually experiencing this messy material matters.

Such hinterland conjures a period, conveys the material culture of distant times and places or cultivates an aesthetic effect. To benefit from and succeed within English, pupils need to be readers, to experience catharsis or mimesis at work (Warwick and Speakman, 2018). The power of a plot, of an earlier motif returning, or of pathos, cannot be achieved vicariously by someone else's summary. Bypassing the hinterland of actual literary experience, of literature 'as an important form of aesthetic knowledge' runs the risk not just of arid teaching but of instrumentalism (Sehgal-Cuthbert, 2017, p. 107). English teaching sometimes bypasses its own purposes to such an extent that we see

Key Stage 3 English. Analyse the sequencing: what is each item doing in making reading of a later text achievable?

Y7	Welwyn Wilton Katz, *Beowulf* Kevin Crossley Holland, *Bracelet of Bones*	Chaucer, *The Canterbury Tales* Cynthia Harnett, *The Wool-Pack*	Performance poetry, inc. Nigerian poet, Patience Agbabi (inc. her poetry influenced by Chaucer) and poet pianist Echezonachukwu Nduka	Shakespeare, *A Midsummer Night's Dream*	Shakespeare, 1 sonnet E. Nesbit, *The Railway Children*	Shakespeare, 1 sonnet Mary Renault, *Fire From Heaven*
Independent reading for pleasure	Henrietta Branford, *Fire, Bed and Bone*	Catherine Bruton, *No Ballet Shoes in Syria*	Judith Kerr, *When Hitler Stole Pink Rabbit*		Mandy Hartley, *The DNA Detectives*	Fleur Hitchcock, *The Boy who Flew*
Y8	Renaissance poetry inc. Spenser, *The Faerie Queene* Rosemary Sutcliff, *Song for a Dark Queen*	Shakespeare, *Julius Caesar* Rukiya Khatun, 'My Mother Country' Dryden, *Annus Mirabilis*	Poetry, place & perspective: Clare Holtham, *The Road from Herat*	Romantic poetry (inc Byron, Wordsworth, Coleridge, Shelley, Keats, Rosetti, Barrett Browning) Early feminist writing: Mary Wollstonecraft Charlotte Bronte, *Jane Eyre*	Wordsworth,	Charles Dickens, *A Tale of Two Cities* Direct and indirect moral persuasion Greta Thunberg Fables
Independent reading for pleasure	Penelope Lively, *The Ghost of Thomas Kempe*		Chinua Achebe, *Things Fall Apart*		Harper Lee, *To Kill a Mocking Bird*	
Y9	WWI poetry, inc. Gurney, Owen, Sassoon. War poetry set to music e.g. American civil war: Walt Whitman, *The Wound-Dresser* (John Adams, music)	Satire in WWI: *The Wipers Times* Early 20C American environment writing (non-fiction), inc: Mary Austin, *The Land of Little Rain*	Kazuo Ishiguro, *The Remains of the Day*	Shakespeare, *The Tempest* (also in Y9 drama; and is whole-school drama production end Spring 2)	20C British Isles poetry, inc. Ted Hughes, RS Thomas, Eluned Phillips, Carol Ann Duffy, Ben Okri; Seamus Heaney. Michael Frayn, *Copenhagen* Modern environment writing (non-fiction) by Robert Macfarlane	Ahdaf Soueif, *The Map of Love* Conveying time & perspective in poetry: Gwendolyn Brooks, Ivor Gurney, Rukiya Khatun
Independent reading for pleasure	George Orwell, *Nineteen Eighty-Four* The chapters on Elizabeth Blackwell and Josephine Butler in Margaret Forster, *Significant Sisters*	George Orwell, *Animal Farm* L.P. Hartley, *The Go-Between*				Kazuo Ishiguro, *Artist of the Floating World* Summer holiday read for all prior to Year 10: Aldous Huxley, *Brave New World*

Figure 2a

the sad irony of pupils trained to answer the ubiquitous examination question, 'What is the effect on the reader...?' without a hope of the text having had an effect on the reader. Humanities teachers isolate the facts in a narrative on a knowledge organiser and forget that experiencing the narrative itself is essential both for retention and for understanding the subject's forms of accounting.

The detail, the drama, the slow work of the symphony, each stage of the novel – these are all necessary for the subject to do its transformative work.

Principle 4: Interpret each subject curriculum through its debates about content scope

How and why might SLT helpfully concern themselves with the nurture of subject breadth when they are not subject specialists?

In those subjects structured more cumulatively than hierarchically and therefore higher in semantic gravity, departments must select from potentially infinite content. Many national curricula (such as England's) specify neither case studies in geography, nor texts in English, nor artistic works. Content choice will always have a complex relationship with changing culture and shifting subject community traditions. Because content choice is bound up with questions of value, identity and purpose, it will be of critical concern to all stakeholders.

For those teachers passionate about their subjects, this goes deeper still. In some subjects, the debates about content choice are so open and alive that to engage in them defines the very essence of being a secondary subject teacher. Which book? Which art? Which culture? Which themes to link, enliven and tease out underlying structures? Even where a curriculum has been borrowed or bought in, the evaluative impulse fosters curricular reasoning about content scope. Would pupils have recognised Y had they tackled more X? Would they have cared more about X or made this connection had they journeyed *via* a richer content route?

Whether such a culture of debating content scope is thriving is very much in the power of SLT, but only if the systemic factors driving its presence or absence are understood. Consider these scenarios possible in English, humanities and the arts.

In scenario 1, a department is locked in instrumentalist solutions. Instead of discussing the value, means and measure of breadth, the department asks, 'How few topics can we get away with?' or 'How can we short-cut to GCSE?' Let us imagine that SLT directly challenges the misapprehension underlying this. Through training, they show the relationship between content breadth and better results: how range of material at KS3 transforms speed and flexibility of comprehension. But a root problem – the systemic problem of professional culture and capacity – is not solved. For while the argument that breadth serves eventual examination outcomes will help, it does not strike at the root problem because it replaces one form of instrumentalism with another.

In scenario 2, the offer is unacceptably narrow in different ways. It may be stuck in monocultural perspectives, in stale canons of art or literature, in topics betraying outdated scholarship or else constrained by what Warwick and Speakman describe as the 'tyranny of relevance' to teenage culture (2018, p. 5). The causes could be various – lack of training, time, resources, knowledge or engagement with subject community. SLT knows what it must fix in the teachers themselves: a transformation of desire, conception and means of breadth. It will probably require outside specialist input. But once outside subject help is sought, how does SLT sustain evolution? How does it keep management conversation focused on what matters?

In scenario 3, the deficit is SLT's. Imagine a subject curriculum that is powerful in scholarly connection and cultural vibrancy, all optimised through coherence and thoroughness. Traditional canons are thoroughly taught, thoroughly challenged and juxtaposed with diverse perspectives. Appreciation fostered in pupils is wide and fruitful. Structural principles recur purposefully, illuminating new content and enabling composition or argument. But the department is frustrated because its curriculum quality is never properly discussed with SLT. The department does not feel known by SLT. The department feels thwarted by whole-school initiatives which are at best redundant and at worst distorting the very strengths SLT ought to celebrate.

In each of these scenarios, SLT's problem is how to interrogate content scope and how to sustain such interrogation so that curriculum strengths or improvements are understood, so that observed teaching is interpreted through its curriculum features, and so that data allows SLT to be usefully forensic.

A key to shaping middle-senior leader conversations about scope lies in the relationship between a curriculum and a domain. A subject curriculum is not the whole subject domain (Koretz, 2008). Its purpose is to give meaningful access to that domain – its field, its questions, its distinctive powers in describing, interpreting and questioning the world. Following this logic, any old 'breadth' and 'richness' won't do. Breadth or richness must derive as much from subject coherence as from wide-ranging topics. The following five questions illustrate ways to unlock this.

1) **What makes this subject's field of enquiry distinctive?**

For example, Standish (2017) explains how geography is different from environmental studies or economics because its questions relate to space:

> Economists aim for an understanding of how economies work and function while geographers study economic activity to understand how it is arranged and connected spatially ... [and] related to other geographical phenomena. (2018, p. 97)

Watch out for merely adding topics without seeing the threads such as spatial connection.

2) **How does breadth create usable frameworks?**

A history department situates England's Norman Conquest within the wider Norman diaspora, including a mini-depth on Norman Sicily – that extraordinary period of Jewish, Muslim and Christian cross-cultural flourishing. Later in year 7, they compare early 14th-century North Africa with English expansion into Wales and Scotland. Alongside a spine of secure chronology and connected narratives, this breadth provides illuminating thoroughness for expansion and empire, themes which become gateways to other content and recurring historical questions. Already, frameworks are building that give interpretative shape to new material, which pupils can later flex and critique.

3) **How do the trade-offs work within a content matrix?**

The English plan in figure 2a is like a multi-dimensional matrix. Its authors have conceptualised scope along several parameters. The scheme weaves chronological journeys with themes (migration, environment, time, place, perspective) that disrupt that chronology. All this is woven with global reference, gender balance (50% female authors) and diversity across the British Isles. Beyond voice and theme, we see continuities in genre, plot device and style. Thus richness multiplies through coherence. Yet no thread in this tapestry can be pure or entire: one is broken to make way for another and this is a strength because the effect of the whole is not calculable by its inputs. SLT must ask what is being sacrificed to what, and why, so the intent is understood.

4) **What are the intrinsic reasons for breadth in this subject?**

It is a sad comment on oversight of arts education that many leave school having studied music, art and literature for a decade without a sense of the great sweep of space and time, a familiar frame of reference to enjoy diverse genres in gallery, concert hall or library. McPhail (2017) discusses the balance between music chosen to foster wide appreciation and music chosen to feed technical accomplishment. In music, art and literature, it is easy to lose sight of the former as a goal in its own right.

Without awareness of the parameters of such debates, an SLT cannot authentically articulate a wider, whole-school line on content scope, nor appreciate conditions for teachers' sustained conversation concerning it (see principle 6), nor avoid the danger of seeking scope by mere accretion.

Principle 5: Understand the role and nurture of a pupil's own judgement, argument or response, within each subject

The production of some form of meaningful judgement, whether disciplinary argument or authentic response to the arts, is an intrinsic part of certain subjects.

First, it forms one part of the curricular **means** of progressing through the domain. We can't gain the benefits of English literature just from listening to teachers' or critics' analyses of novels; we must read novels ourselves in order to feel their power. We can't make sense of history as a discipline only by reading historians' arguments and analysing their features; we come to understand the purpose and process of those arguments by engaging dialogically with them. It would be unthinkable for certain subjects not to include certain intersubjective activities such as these.

Second, such authentic response is treated as a key **measure** of achievement in mastering the domain. Pupils write a paragraph analysing a poem or answer an historical question in the form of an argument.

And this is where the trouble starts. That measure becomes a high-stakes performance. Cue perverse incentives to replicate its surface features, rather than going the long way round. In the English example above, going the long way round means reading whole novels, plenty of them, having time to talk about responses to them, and reading more. It means getting close to the point of the subject which is to be constantly changed by the new worlds we acquire as we move through a novel at the pace of the novel, and the new conversations we have with others who have read the same. In the history example, going the long

111

way round means learning to argue properly, and about historical questions that really matter because they concern everyone's responsibility to question the warrant of claims about the past.

Relevant cognitive science ought to help here, for it teaches that performance differs from learning. Performance is underpinned by secure schemata or mental models, the webs of connected reference that frame all that we subsequently interpret, changing the patterns we discern (Feltovich et al., 2006). Christodoulou summarises the implication:

> Performance depends on the detailed, knowledge-rich mental models stored in long-term memory. The aim of performance is to use those mental models. The aim of learning is to create them. The activities which create those models often don't look like the performance itself. (2017, p. 43)

Getting distracted by the performance is common in this instance, for the performance is easy to conflate with a particular kind of writing that will pass muster in a particular assessment context. Before we know it, pupils are being taught formulae for paragraph structures or to include certain terms at all costs. Sometimes, in a particularly unfortunate perversion, cognitive science around long-term memory is itself invoked to justify endless rehearsal of a particular sentence stem standing in for judgement. Rehearsing given causes in history is deemed the required 'practice'. The mental models gained from extensive encounters with literature or the genuine practice in facets of historical argument – the learning that the assessment is really designed to test – are missed altogether.

Let us be clear about what is going wrong here, why it is so serious and why it is a curricular matter of concern to high-level leadership. Fundamental purposes and experiences of learning the subject are being missed (weakening preparation for the test, to boot). In English, instead of the wide, first-hand knowledge of texts that would have underpinned authentic response, the performance features of writing are taught as generic, procedural skills. In the history example, historical argument has been proceduralised to such an extent that no argument is required. Instead, pupils memorise whole arguments or lists of pre-packaged 'causes', the very thing that proper training in causal argument would have taught them cannot exist.

SLT have responsibility for nurturing a professional culture of attending to the proper purposes of subjects and proper means of progressing through the domain. Just two questions can unlock this. 1) What is authentic pupil judgement *doing* in this subject? i.e. what is its role in the domain? 2) What kind of curricular journey makes it possible over time? Answers will diverge widely, for each school version of a subject stands in a slightly different relationship to its real-world, scholarly or artistic practices and products.

In English, the journey can only be undertaken by painstakingly building the mental models that make the difference. Challenging the short-termism of many schools' approaches to English teaching, Bleiman (2020) insists that independent response will not come cheaply and its counterfeit is not worth having. Novels must be read in their entirety, pupils must experience a rich, wide range and they must gain the experience of living inside a book, rather than using it as a setting for constant skill practice. This is their *knowledge*. Poetry requires,

> ...a sense of what is possible across the whole genre, absorbing insights by many encounters with a variety of poems. It's deeply and unavoidably intertextual. You want a ballad or a sonnet is and its parameters by reading several. If a poet stretches or subverts conventions, you only know that by familiarity with several examples. (Bleiman, 2020, p. 150)

Some might argue that getting lower attainers to read whole novels is prohibitively difficult, but recent research challenges such defeatism. Westbrook et al. (2019) trialled an approach designed to give low attainers the experience of uninterrupted reading by prioritising the reading of two full novels over 12 weeks. They found students made 8.5 months' mean progress on standardised comprehension tests, with the hitherto poorer readers making 16 months' progress.

In history, after plenty of exposure to real debates, broad knowledge and careful support in reasoning, pupils eventually learn that 'causes' are not pre-existing; they are constituted. Production of a causal argument is not the sum of memorising things called 'causes'. We must memorise relevant facts but turning them into causes is a matter of argument.

These two examples illustrate how proper understanding of the role of pupils' own responses leads us to their proper nurture. If pupil response is confused with procedural skill or the memorisation of superficial performance features, not only is the performance fragile but pupils have missed out on the essence and joy of the subject that was meant to give them new voice – getting lost in novels and having proper historical arguments.

Principle 6: Understand the role of particular subject communities in the development of teachers as curricular thinkers

Underlying all the above is the reality that a school's core activity – knowledge, expertise and the life of the mind – looks to loci of authority outside of school: the knowledge practices renewed in subject communities. Curricula are not static, neutral conduits, packaged in textbook and specification. Curricula will be strong in intent and implementation where teachers have a dynamic relationship to the knowledge that they teach. A challenge for SLT is that these subject communities differ widely in nature and role. For SLT to understand how they can serve curriculum development requires awareness of the *kinds* of debates taking place in these communities and their interplay with teacher development.

One way through this is to think about subject teachers engaging with subject communities on two levels. The first level is the direct relationship to disciplinary or artistic practices. It would be unthinkable to imagine an English department developing as teachers, let alone collaborating as curriculum thinkers, without reading novels, watching plays, discussing poetry and engaging with traditions of critique. If, when they become teachers, music teachers stopped listening to and making music, neither effective music teaching nor informed music curricula would survive. History teachers whose reading and discussion of historical scholarship stopped aged 22 are history teachers stuck in a time warp, ill-equipped to model the vibrancy and rigour of continuing historical debate or to weigh content. But what is the equivalent in science? Is sustaining engagement with science journals so fundamental to science teachers' professional drive and curriculum quality? If not, is there an equivalent type of direct engagement, with different powers?

The second level is subject *education* communities. These might include subject teachers, subject education researchers or teacher-trainers, operate with varying degrees of formality (subject associations or more diffuse communities) and may or may not produce a coherent discourse shaping collective professional knowledge. Working out whether a subject department is adequately engaged with a strong subject community can prove a minefield for SLT. But a key acid test is this: do your subject teachers understand the really big debates that inform all subsequent discourse? A history teacher trying to use recent, influential work on causal argument will be far less likely to waste time reinventing round or square wheels and will find current teachers' writing (e.g. Stanford, 2019; Foster and Goudie, 2019) much more illuminating if they already know about the earlier curricular breakthroughs of history teachers to which these recent pieces refer (e.g. Woodcock, 2005). A reading of Warwick and Speakman (2018) on new directions for knowledge in English is greatly helped by knowing the contours of English education debates about literature and society (e.g. Holbrook, 1979).

The second level frequently engages productively with the first. When exploring disciplinary concepts for geography, Bustin (2011) drew on geographical scholarship to frame his teaching of urban social issues through the concept of space. A marked trend in the last decade of history teachers' publications in England has been use of historical scholarship to drive curriculum planning and research (Foster, 2016; Jenner, 2019).

We know that teachers' engagement with subject curricular challenges is bound up with their drive for self-improvement (Brooks, 2016; Burn, 2016; Healy, 2019), making it unsurprising that recent research should find a link between teacher autonomy and teacher recruitment and retention (Worth and Van den Brande, 2020). Conversely, departments locked in instrumentalist solutions, narrow offers and outdated scholarship – or departments who *do* thrive on sustained engagement with subject communities but fear that this is not valued by SLT – may struggle to attract or retain strong subject teachers for whom serious intellectual subject engagement is both a core professional responsibility (Cordingley et al., 2018) and part of the joyful sense of agency in being a subject teacher (e.g. Olivey, 2019; Kueh, 2020). An SLT uninterested in this relationship of teachers to their sources of knowledge will find it hard to 'read' a curriculum, to understand the loci of authority to which good subject leaders appeal or to judge the value of particular professional development for curriculum quality.

Shaping management conversations: Three sites of transformation

In what practical contexts can a senior leader gain and use these understandings? I conclude with three examples of routine, professional interactions that illustrate the logic of placing curriculum at the centre of management conversations: questions about substance triggering further and better questions about substance. Each is dependent on dialogue. The moment each becomes a checklist, a tool to make things tidy for SLT, management convenience has usurped the very construct that the structure was designed to exemplify. Being led by substance of subject, using the six principles above, is one antidote to this.

Conversation 1: a department's discussion

Figure 2b illustrates a curricular discussion one might expect to see in a department meeting that is keeping a strong curriculum (such as that in figure

A head of English's plan for an English department meeting designed to keep the sequencing in Figure 2a under review

1. Let's review the sequencing rationale of the following elements:

- The positioning of each Year 7 item: are we still happy with our rationale for the proximal role of each within Year 7?
- The position of L.P. Hartley, *The Go Between*. We placed certain novels prior to it in order to improve access to this novel for all Year 9. Did we get that right? What, from experience of reading of these earlier stories, has indirectly resonated for the pupil in style, content, tone, period detail, allusions, sentence structure, voice ..., helping to make *The Go Between* feel readable, interesting and compelling?
- The positioning of Shakespeare's *Julius Caesar*. Does our experience bear out it being in the right place, or should we move it?
- Together with SLT, we agreed that reading Aldous Huxley's *Brave New World* must be a core, foundational cultural experience for the whole school. We decided that pupils' ability to find it fascinating and to use it as a source of critical debate about technology and ethics in other subjects in Years 10 to 13, and about dystopian writing in English, will be one measure of the success of our KS3 English programme. Our goal is to make this a reality for a minimum of 90% of pupils. [Remaining 10% of pupils will be carefully supported through an abridged version, in a lunchtime Y9 reading club, so that no pupil lacks BNW as a reference point.) Which six texts from our Years 7 to 9 programme have played the part that we hoped in ensuring all are ready for independent enjoyment of Huxley by Year 10?

2. What has been the impact of studying a Shakespeare play and Shakespeare's sonnets in Year 7 within pupils' response to:

- the study of Shakespeare and Spenser in Year 8?
- the study of Romantic poetry in Year 9?
- all poetry studies in Year 9?
- our Elizabeth Barrett Browning sonnets in Year 11?

3. Two of you have suggested replacing Robert Macfarlane with Ronald Blythe's *Akenfield*. Purely in the context of sequencing rationale, let's consider:

- What might be the advantages and disadvantages in such a switch in terms of the reading we would want pupils to access later (at GCSE, A Level or wider general reading for pleasure)?
- What earlier texts (Years 7 & 8, and early Year 9) might show their impact on pupils more readily in their response to Robert Macfarlane than they would in their response to Blythe? How might Akenfield warm up, consolidate and provide new reflection on topics typically covered in Year 9 history?

4. How far does our programme ensure all students are ready to access any novels in any future English GCSEs and are likely to read widely for pleasure, in world fiction, beyond age 16? Think of diverse novelists from Tolstoy to Zola, from Nabukov to Naipaul, from Achebe to Aslan. Think Morrison, Ghosh, Atwood, Smith, as well as Eliot, Gaskell, Hardy and Austen. Should/Could any of our KS3 texts be changed without unravelling too much of the current sequencing rationale?

from: Christine Counsell, SLT seminar: what is curriculum doing in your theory of school improvement?

Figure 2b

2a) under review. It is presented as questions a head of English might use to drive curriculum review, while simultaneously developing the department's knowledge and curricular thinking.

To observe such a meeting even just once a term allows senior leader to be led by the object of concern – the subject itself.

Conversation 2: senior-middle leader management conversation

Figure 3a illustrates a flow of questions for furnishing a routine management conversation between senior and middle leader, a conversation that is trying both to uncover curriculum itself and to apply subject-specific curricular understandings to visible expressions of it – classroom teaching, students' work, assessment data, evaluative exercises and departmental meetings. Figure 3b shows how such questions start to look in a particular subject context, as the conversation between senior and middle leaders matures through sustained nurture.

Curriculum intent	Curriculum implementation	Curriculum impact
1. What big ideas / wider trends/ general principles is x part of?	1. What blend of teaching approaches do you expect to see if pupils are to gain mastery of x?	1. How confident are you that pupils remember what they have been taught about x? What is typical evidence of this (a) in lessons? (b) in subsequent pieces of work?
2. What is a sign that a pupil has been properly educated in this subject by the time they drop it in Y9 or Y11? What will they recognise easily and/or enjoy and/or be able to do?	2. What does a clear account, explanation or story look like in your subject? 3. How well do teachers keep pupils focused on big idea/ central Q/ disciplinary problem across a particular lesson sequence?	2. How does mastery of x surface in later, different work? 3. From looking at things pupils find hard in Ys 10 & 11, what can you deduce about what pupils need more of in Ys7 & 8? (think background components that will result in better underlying prep for GCSE before Year 10; NOT exam practice, GCSE questions etc).
3. What prior reference points (previous week, month, term, year?) will be enabling pupils to tackle this new topic/issue/concept without overloading working memory?	4. Why has this resource been designed in this way? 5. What subject-specific development does your department need (be precise; think long-term, substantial, sustainable improvement). 6. Show me the package of formative assessment approaches that allow you to check x is secure in pupils' memories.	4. What does high-quality composition (English, art, music) or problem-solving (science, humanities, maths) look like? What earlier curriculum components made this possible?
4. What broad, recurring vocab/ themes/ principles will this detail in Year 7/8/9 render secure in Year 11?	7. What do pupils spend time practising when learning about x? 8. What do pupils write about x in their books? 9. What kinds of examples of x do pupils learn about or practise?	5. Analyse the weaknesses in x work in Y10. Which underlying curriculum components need to be more prevalent/ better sequenced/ more thoroughly taught back in Ys 7, 8, 9?
5. When will pupils revisit x in future?	10. Which pupils may struggle with x and how are you tackling this?	6. How does the quality of the work we produce on x compare with that of subject departments in other schools as evidenced in subject professional publications?

Figure 3a

History curriculum intent	History curriculum implementation	History curriculum impact
1. Why have you chosen to teach Y7 pupils about the 12th century Renaissance through John of Salisbury's story? 2. What are the main 'takeaways' you want Y7 pupils to have at the end of their 6-lesson sequence on the 12th century Renaissance? 3. Which disciplinary principle are you getting at in your 'enquiry question', "Where did the 12th century Renaissance take place?" (What is the open-ended aspect of that Qu? What type of historical problem will they be trying to solve)? 4. How will secure knowledge of the 12th century Renaissance alter Y7's readiness to tackle (a) the Y7 Easter Term topic on heresy and humanism; (b) the Y7 Summer Term topic on the Reformation?	1. Which staff are sufficiently secure in their knowledge of medieval religious reform and which need more knowledge and confidence? How are you building that knowledge and confidence? 2. What formative assessment do you expect your staff to use during this unit? 3. What will be the signs, in the teaching of this unit, that teachers are using adequate 'hinterland' knowledge to support the core takeaways?	1. Show me evidence that 'takeaways' you intended Y7 pupils to have at the end of their 6-lesson sequence on the 12th century Renaissance are surfacing in later written work. 2. What is the evidence in (a) Mrs Blogg's spring term lessons on heresy and humanism; (b) Mr Scroggs summer term lessons on the Reformation that pupils' prior learning of the 12th century Renaissance was effective in its aims?

Figure 3b

What will you see in geography lessons?	What will you see in pupils' geography books?
Students will work with a variety of **geographical sources** (images, texts, statistical data, graphical data, maps). They will always be shown how to use them and will be required to recall and compare earlier use of them. GIS will be used for visualisation and spatial analysis of geographical information. Geography teachers will read **extended tests aloud** (textbook, news articles, journal extracts) with students. Teachers will have pre-taught most relevant Tier 2/3 vocabulary. Choral response is used for new T2/3 vocabulary. **Explanation, modelling and questioning:** We aim for security in the specified content and explicit reflection on the role of space, place and scale (as relevant) in shaping the relevant geographical thinking (eg making links, building synthesis, shaping hypotheses, establishing relationships etc)	Written answers to questions/tasks: short answers ranging from a few sentences to a paragraph.. Geographical T2/3 vocabulary will be appropriately deployed within this writing. Exercises in which students hypothesise and then check hypotheses using geographical data and other sources. Longer, synoptic tasks: students will complete independent extended work every half term. Modelling, scaffolding and redrafting will be punctuated with whole-class discussion fostering geographical thinking.
What formative assessment will you see in geography? Written and oral quick quizzes will be routinely used check recall of key places, landforms, processes and concepts that students need to have at their fingertips. Zoomed in 'topic' maps and timelines from memory at strategic points to check recall of topic knowledge relevant to current topic. Students will write short paragraphs in response to geographical questions inviting recall and application of geographical knowledge and thinking. This will sometimes be applied to *new* case study material. This will be used to test indirect manifestation of knowledge: e.g. How is **globalisation** affecting x? Why would cold environments have such low **biodiversity**?	**What is the department currently reading and discussing, and why?** **We are currently reading:** Bustin, R. (2011) 'The living city: Thirdspace and the contemporary geography curriculum', Geography 96 (2). Soja, E. (1996) Thirdspace, Oxford: Blackwell. **Why?** We are comparing our current use of the concept of 'space' with Soja's and using the published work of a practising geography teacher, Bustin, who has done similar.

Figure 4

Conversation 3: translating the subject – a tool for non-specialist observers

Figure 4 is an example of a device produced by a subject specialist to show a non-specialist senior leader what they should ideally see in lessons. It effectively says, 'Observing teachers teaching or pupils learning geography, you should see this. This is what it means in geographical terms. This is the part it plays in the ongoing narrative of geography education. This is a sign it is working optimally. This is a sign it has gone off course.'

Conclusion

What is gained when such conversations take curriculum as their currency? First, they shift away from a checking-up process or 'review' designed to satisfy a management narrative and become, instead, a serious engagement informed by the subject. Second, the opportunity for earlier diagnosis of serious problems is raised. Third, whole-school analysis of what pupils are actually learning, overall, might finally be possible.

References

Bauckham, I. (2016) *Modern foreign languages pedagogy review*. Teaching Schools Council.

Bleiman, B. (2020) *What matters in English teaching*. London: English and Media Centre.

Brooks, C. (2016) *Teacher subject identity in professional practice: teaching with a professional compass*. Abingdon: Routledge.

Brooks, C. (2018) 'How do we understand conceptual development in school geography?' in Jones, M. and Lambert, D. (eds) *Debates in geography teaching*. London: Routledge, pp. 75–88.

Burn, K. (2016) 'Sustaining the unresolving tensions within history education and teacher education', in Counsell, C., Burn, K. and Chapman, A. (eds) *Masterclass in history education: transforming teaching and learning*. London: Bloomsbury, pp. 233–242.

Brown, G. and Burnham, S. (2004) 'Assessment after levels', *Teaching History* 157 (1) pp. 8–17.

Bustin, R. (2011) 'The living city: Thirdspace and the contemporary geography curriculum', *Geography* 96 (2) pp. 60–68.

Christodoulou, D. (2017) *Making good progress? The future of assessment for learning*. Oxford: Oxford University Press.

Cordingley, P., Greany, T., Crisp, B., Seleznyov, S., Bradbury, M. and Perry, T. (2018) *Developing great subject teaching: rapid evidence review of subject-specific continuing professional development in the UK*. London: Wellcome Trust.

Counsell, C. (2018) 'Senior curriculum leadership 1: the indirect manifestation of knowledge: (A) curriculum as narrative', *The Dignity of the Thing* [Blog], 7 April. Retrieved from: www.bit.ly/2KEr2eW

Feltovich, P. J., Prietula, M. J. and Ericsson, K. A. (2006) 'Studies of expertise from psychological perspectives' in Ericsson, K. A., Charness, N., Feltovich, P. J. and Hoffman, R. R. (eds) *The*

Cambridge handbook of expertise and expert performance. Cambridge: Cambridge University Press, pp. 41–67.

Fordham, M. (2020a) 'The importance of subject leadership – or, why do we need more Giles Fullards?', *Clio et cetera* [Blog], 7 February. Retrieved from: www.bit.ly/2WAXBiw

Fordham, M. (2020b) 'How useful are generic educational ideas?', *Clio et cetera* [Blog], 9 March. Retrieved from: www.bit.ly/2WxZUmE

Foster, R. (2016) 'Historical change: in search of argument' in Counsell, C., Burn, K. and Chapman, A. (eds) *Masterclass in history education: transforming teaching and learning.* London: Bloomsbury, pp. 5–22.

Foster, R. and Goudie, K. (2019) 'a b c D e? Teaching year 9 to take on the challenge of structure in narrative', *Teaching History* 175 (1) pp. 28–39.

Healy, G. (2019) 'Subject scholarship as a mechanism for developing trainees' reflective practice and teachers' curricular thinking', *Impact* 6. Retrieved from: www.bit.ly/3c8PzUB.

Holbrook, D. (1979) *English for meaning.* Slough: NFER.

Jackson, P. (2006) 'Thinking geographically', *Geography* 91 (3) pp. 199–204.

Jenner, T. (2019) 'Making reading routine: helping key stage 3 pupils to become regular readers of historical scholarship', *Teaching History* 174 (1) pp. 42–48.

Kirschner, P. A. (2002) 'Cognitive load theory: implications of cognitive load theory on the design of learning', *Learning and Instruction* 12 (1) pp. 1–10.

Koretz, D. (2008) *Measuring up: what educational testing really tells us.* Cambridge, MA: Harvard University Press.

Kueh, R. (2020) 'Towards subject leadership in religion and worldviews: a plea for subject plenipotentiaries' in Chater, M. (ed.) *Reforming religious education: power and knowledge in a worldviews curriculum.* Woodbridge: John Catt Educational, pp. 131–147.

Lambert, D. (2017) 'Thinking geographically' in Jones, M. (ed.) *Handbook of secondary geography.* Sheffield: Geographical Association, pp. 22–39.

Lambert, D. and Morgan, J. (2010) *Teaching geography 11–18: a conceptual approach.* Maidenhead: Open University Press.

McPhail, G. (2017) 'Powerful knowledge: insights from music's case', *The Curriculum Journal* 28 (4) pp. 524–538.

Maton, K. (2014) *Knowledge and knowers: towards a realist sociology of education.* London: Routledge.

Olivey, J. (2019) 'What did "class" mean to a Chartist? Teaching year 8 pupils to take seriously the ideas of ordinary people from the past', *Teaching History* 176 (1) pp. 60–71.

Qualifications and Curriculum Authority (2007) *The national curriculum: geography.* Department for Education. London: The Stationery Office. Retrieved from: www.bit.ly/3bceqWi

Rata, E. (2019) 'Knowledge-rich teaching: a model of curriculum design coherence', *British Educational Research Journal* 45 (4) pp. 681–697.

Rosenshine, B. (2012) 'Principles of instruction: research-based strategies that all teachers should know', *American Educator* 36 (1) pp. 12–19, 39.

Sehgal-Cuthbert, A. (2017) 'English literature' in Standish, A. and Sehgal-Cuthbert, A. (eds) *What should schools teach? Disciplines, subjects and the pursuit of truth.* London: UCL Institute of Education Press, pp. 104–120.

Standish, A. (2017) 'Geography' in Standish, A. and Sehgal-Cuthbert, A. (eds) *What should schools teach? Disciplines, subjects and the pursuit of truth.* London: UCL Institute of Education Press, pp. 88–103.

Stanford, M. (2019) 'Did the Bretons break? Planning increasingly complex causal models at key stage 3', *Teaching History* 175 (1) pp. 8–15.

Stanton, S. (2019) 'Curriculum conversations: art', *The Dusty Tsundoku* [Blog], 5 June. Retrieved from: www.bit.ly/2L6pDNO

Taylor, L. (2008) 'Key concepts and medium-term planning', *Teaching Geography* 33 (2) pp. 50–54.

Walker, R. (2018) 'The nature of school science knowledge and why Adam's SLT was wrong', *The Fruits Are Sweet* [Blog], 14 January. Retrieved from: www.bit.ly/2SEFs2a

Warwick, I. and Speakman, R. (2018) *Redefining English for the more able: a practical guide.* London: Routledge.

Westbrook, J., Sutherland, J., Oakhill, J. and Sullivan, S. (2019) 'Just reading: increasing pace and volume of reading whole narratives on the comprehension of poorer adolescent readers in English classrooms', *Literacy* 53 (2) pp. 60–68.

Woodcock, J. (2005) 'Does the linguistic release the conceptual? Helping year 10 to improve their causal reasoning' in *Teaching History* 119 (1) pp. 5–14.

Worth, J. and Van den Brande, J. (2020) *Teacher autonomy: how does it relate to job satisfaction and retention?* Slough: NFER.

Author bio-sketch:

Christine Counsell is a freelance education consultant who has been teacher, senior leader, local authority adviser, teacher trainer, senior lecturer at the University of Cambridge and Director of Education of a MAT. She has worked nationally and internationally, supporting policy makers, scholars, leaders and teachers, and specialising in the teaching of history in post-conflict zones. Christine was a member of the Ofsted Curriculum Advisory Group and the DfE Workload Solutions group. She serves on the boards of the David Ross Education Trust, Now Teach and Ark Curriculum Partnerships. Editor of the Historical Association's journal *Teaching History*, she has published widely.